SOCKS
TO KNIT
for those you love

LEISURE ARTS, INC.
Little Rock, Akransas

Want to warm your loved ones right down to their toes? Hand-knitted socks are the most thoughtful of gifts, and are always welcome! Renowned designer and instructor Edie Eckman offers these 18 styles for the family. Simple or fancy, cabled or lacy, they range from wee baby booties to roomy socks for men. Thorough instructions include all the stitches and techniques you'll need, including Edie's helpful pattern stitch charts. And with the huge array of yarn colors available, your socks are sure to be the right fit for the lucky recipient!

TABLE OF CONTENTS

EDITORIAL STAFF
Editor-in-Chief: Susan White Sullivan
Knit and Crochet Publications Director: Lindsay White Glenn
Director of Designer Relations: Cheryl Johnson
Special Projects Director: Susan Frantz Wiles
Senior Prepress Director: Mark Hawkins
Art Publications Director: Rhonda Shelby
Technical Writer/Editor: Cathy Hardy
Contributing Editors: Linda A. Daley, Sarah J. Green,
    and Lois J. Long
Editorial Writer: Susan McManus Johnson
Art Category Manager: Lora Puls
Graphic Artists: Dana Vaughn and Becca Snider
Imaging Technician: Stephanie Johnson
Prepress Technician: Janie Marie Wright
Photography Manager: Katherine Laughlin
Contributing Photographers: Jason Masters and Ken West
Contributing Photo Stylists: Sondra Daniel and Brooke Deszota
Publishing Systems Administrator: Becky Riddle
Mac Information Technology Specialist: Robert Young

BUSINESS STAFF
President and Chief Executive Officer: Rick Barton
Vice President of Sales: Mike Behar
Director of Finance and Administration: Laticia Mull Dittrich
National Sales Director: Martha Adams
Creative Services: Chaska Lucas
Information Technology Director: Hermine Linz
Controller: Francis Caple
Vice President, Operations: Jim Dittrich
Retail Customer Service Manager: Stan Raynor
Print Production Manager: Fred F. Pruss

Library of Congress Control Number: 2011930886

ISBN-13: 978-1-60900-226-8

Meet the multitalented
EDIE ECKMAN

Years ago, Edie Eckman co-owned a yarn shop. The work severely limited her time to knit and crochet, so she closed the shop after a while and turned to designing.

"Now I have my fingers in many aspects of the fiber arts," Edie says. She teaches her popular workshops at Stitches events, the National Needlearts Association, Crochet Guild of America and The Knitting Guild of America conferences and other national venues, as well as at local shops and guilds. "I love the 'a-ha' moment when a student gains a new bit of understanding," she says.

Edie also freelances as a technical editor for yarn craft magazines and writes best-selling books on knitting and crochet. Her many titles include *Fresh Vests to Knit* (a Leisure Arts book), *The Crochet Answer Book*, and *Around the Corner Crochet Borders*.

"My family is very supportive of my travel-heavy life," Edie says. "My husband and our two children assist me by helping around the house while I stitch, pack, and prepare classes."

When developing knitting and crochet patterns, Edie doesn't design "on the needles or on the hook."

"Occasionally," she says, "a design pops fully formed into my head, but most of my creative process happens when I'm swatching. The fabric I create generates ideas. The finished swatch serves as my guide for sketching, pattern drafting, and stitching a sample."

Even before her design career was established, Edie had faith in her creative instincts.

"My most challenging knitting project was a multi-colored intarsia vest designed by Sasha Kagan," says Edie. "It was twenty-six years ago. I had knit only two sweaters in my life, and those were just one color. Off I bopped to the yarn shop to buy the fingering weight yarn and the 3.25 mm needles required. If I had asked the shop owner, she would have steered me to something easier based on my experience, but it never occurred to me to ask.

"I struggled to knit that vest and it turned out beautifully. I still have it and show it in some of the classes I teach. To me, it's an example of not letting skill level designations keep you from making what you want. 'Too hard' patterns are a chance to ramp up my knitting skills and push myself to learn faster."

When Edie wants to unplug from her fast-paced work life, she heads for the woods.

"We have a little cabin. There's no TV or Internet service. I love to go there for walks and to paddle around the lake. However, I'm always looking for the next editing job, and I've always got designs in my head, ready to be sold."

To see Edie's workshop schedule, visit her Web site at EdieEckman.com. She can also be found on Facebook as EdieEckman, and there is an Edie Eckman Stitchers group on Ravelry. To get your copy of *Fresh Vests to Knit* (#5261), visit LeisureArts.com.

BRIGHT TWEED SOCKS

Size: Woman
Finished Foot Circumference: 7" (18 cm)
Finished Foot Length: 9¹/₂" (24 cm)

Size Note: These socks can easily be made to fit children ages 10-12 by making the foot length shorter *(see Sizing, page 89).*

MATERIALS

SUPER FINE **1**

Super Fine Weight Yarn
[1.75 ounces, 191 yards
(50 grams, 175 meters) per
hank]:
  A (Red multi) - 2 hanks
  B (Yellow) - 1 hank
Set of 4 double pointed knitting
  needles, size 2 (2.75 mm)
  or size needed for gauge
Split-ring marker
Tapestry needle

GAUGE: In Tweed Stitch,
     16 sts and 30 rnds =
     2" (5 cm)
     in Stockinette Stitch,
     16 sts and 23 rnds =
     2" (5 cm)
✓ *Take the time to check your gauge.*

Techniques used:
- K2 tog *(Fig. 9, page 92)*
- SSK *(Figs. 12a-c, page 92)*
- P2 tog *(Fig. 15, page 93)*

CUFF

With A, cast on 56 sts loosely.

Divide stitches onto 3 needles, arranged 19-18-19.

Place a marker around the first stitch and join for working in the round, being careful not to twist stitches *(see Double Pointed Needles, page 90)*.

Work in K1, P1 ribbing until Sock measures 1½" (4 cm) from cast on edge.

LEG

When instructed to slip a stitch, slip purlwise with yarn in back, unless otherwise specified.

Rnd 1: Knit around.

Rnds 2 and 3: With B, ★ slip 1, K3; repeat from ★ around.

Rnd 4: With A, K2, slip 1, ★ K3, slip 1; repeat from ★ around to last st, K1.

Rnd 5: With A, K2, P1, ★ K3, P1; repeat from ★ around to last st, K1.

Rnds 6 and 7: With B, K2, slip 1, ★ K3, slip 1; repeat from ★ around to last st, K1.

Rnd 8: With A, ★ slip 1, K3; repeat from ★ around.

Rnd 9: With A, ★ P1, K3; repeat from ★ around.

Repeat Rnds 2-9 for Tweed Stitch until Sock measures approximately 6" (15 cm) from cast on edge, ending by working an odd numbered round.

Cut B.

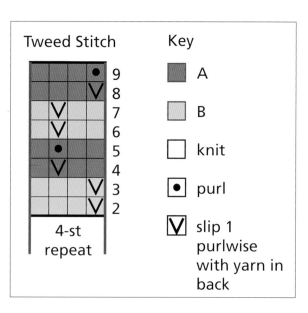

Tweed Stitch — Key: A, B, knit, purl, slip 1 purlwise with yarn in back. 4-st repeat.

HEEL

Dividing Row: Knit across Needle 1, with same needle, knit 9 sts from Needle 2; slip remaining sts from Needle 2 onto Needle 3 and leave these 28 sts unworked for Instep.

The Heel Flap will be worked back and forth in rows across the first 28 stitches.

HEEL FLAP

Row 1 (Wrong side)**:** Slip 1 purlwise with yarn in front, purl across; turn.

Row 2: ★ Slip 1 purlwise with yarn in back, K1; repeat from ★ across; turn.

Repeat Rows 1 and 2, 13 times.

HEEL TURNING

Begin working in short rows as follows:

Row 1 (Wrong side)**:** P 16, P2 tog, P1, leave remaining 9 sts unworked; **turn.**

Continuing to slip the first stitch holding yarn to **wrong** side, slip knitwise on all **right** side rows and purlwise on all **wrong** side rows.

Row 2: Slip 1, K5, SSK, K1; turn.

Row 3: Slip 1, P6, P2 tog, P1; turn.

Row 4: Slip 1, K7, SSK, K1; turn.

Row 5: Slip 1, P8, P2 tog, P1; turn.

Row 6: Slip 1, K9, SSK, K1; turn.

Row 7: Slip 1, P 10, P2 tog, P1; turn.

Row 8: Slip 1, K 11, SSK, K1; turn.

Row 9: Slip 1, P 12, P2 tog, P1; turn.

Row 10: Slip 1, K 13, SSK, K1; turn.

Row 11: Slip 1, P 14, P2 tog; turn.

Row 12: Slip 1, K 14, SSK: 16 sts.

GUSSET

Rnd 1: With **right** side of Heel facing and using needle holding Heel sts (Needle 1), pick up 14 sts along edge of Heel Flap *(Fig. 17, page 93)*, pick up one st in gap between Heel Flap and Instep; with empty needle, knit 28 Instep sts (Needle 2); with empty needle, pick up one st in gap between Instep and Heel Flap, pick up 14 sts along edge of Heel Flap, knit first 8 sts of Heel from Needle 1 (Needle 3), place marker around next st to indicate beginning of rnd: 74 sts, arranged 23-28-23.

Rnd 2 (Decrease rnd)**:** On Needle 1, knit across needle to last 3 sts, K2 tog, K1; on Needle 2, knit across; on Needle 3, K1, SSK, knit across: 72 sts.

Rnd 3: Knit around.

Repeat Rnds 2 and 3, 8 times: 56 sts, arranged 14-28-14.

Continued on page 17.

BRAIDED CABLE SOCKS

∎∎∎◻ INTERMEDIATE

Sizes	Finished Foot Circumference	Finished Foot Length
Woman	7$\frac{1}{2}$" (19 cm)	9$\frac{1}{2}$" (24 cm)
Man	8$\frac{1}{4}$" (21 cm)	11" (28 cm)

Size Note: The Woman's size can easily be made to fit children ages 10-12 by making the foot length shorter *(see Sizing, page 89).* Instructions are written for Woman's size with Man's size in braces { }. Instructions will be easier to read if you circle all the numbers pertaining to your size. If only one number is given, it applies to both sizes.

MATERIALS

SUPER FINE ❶

Super Fine Weight Yarn
[1.76 ounces, 230 yards
(50 grams, 210 meters) per skein]:
  2 skeins
Set of 4 double pointed knitting
  needles, size 2 (2.75 mm) **or** size
  needed for gauge
Split-ring marker
Cable needle
Tapestry needle

GAUGE: In Braided Cable pattern,
  20{22} sts = 2$\frac{1}{2}${2$\frac{3}{4}$}"/
  6.25{7} cm

✓ *Take the time to check your gauge.*

Techniques used:
• K2 tog *(Fig. 9, page 92)*
• SSK *(Figs. 12a-c, page 92)*
• P2 tog *(Fig. 15, page 93)*

STITCH GUIDE

2/2 RC *(2 over 2 Right Cross; uses 4 sts)*
Slip next 2 sts onto cable needle and hold in **back** of work, K2 from left needle, K2 from cable needle.

2/2 LC *(2 over 2 Left Cross; uses 4 sts)*
Slip next 2 sts onto cable needle and hold in **front** of work, K2 from left needle, K2 from cable needle.

BRAIDED CABLE

(multiple of 10{11} sts)
Rnd 1: P2, K6, ★ P4{5}, K6; repeat from ★ around to last 2{3} sts, P2{3}.
Rnd 2: Knit around.
Rnd 3: P2, 2/2 RC, K2, ★ P4{5}, 2/2 RC, K2; repeat from ★ around to last 2{3} sts, P2{3}.
Rnd 4: Knit around.
Rnd 5: P2, K6, ★ P4{5}, K6; repeat from ★ around to last 2{3} sts, P2{3}.
Rnd 6: Knit around.
Rnd 7: P2, K2, 2/2 LC, ★ P4{5}, K2, 2/2 LC; repeat from ★ around to last 2{3} sts, P2{3}.
Rnd 8: Knit around.
Repeat Rnds 1-8 for Braided Cable pattern.

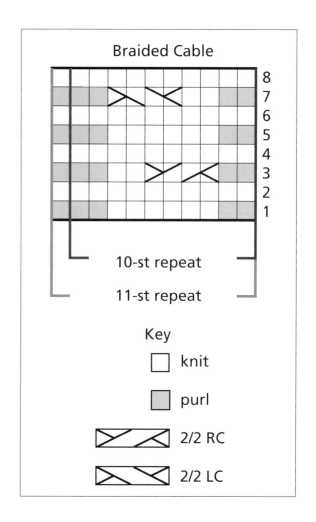

Braided Cable

10-st repeat

11-st repeat

Key

☐ knit

▨ purl

⬚ 2/2 RC

⬚ 2/2 LC

LEG

Cast on 60{66} sts loosely.

Divide stitches onto 3 needles, placing 20{22} on each.

Place a marker around the first stitch and join for working in the round, being careful not to twist stitches *(see Double Pointed Needles, page 90)*.

Work in Braided Cable pattern until Leg measures approximately 6{7}"/ 15{18} cm from cast on edge.

HEEL

Dividing Row: Knit across Needle 1, with same needle, knit 10 sts from Needle 2; slip remaining sts from Needle 2 onto Needle 3 and leave these 30{34} sts unworked for Instep.

The Heel Flap will be worked back and forth in rows across the first 30{32} stitches.

HEEL FLAP

Row 1 (Wrong side): Slip 1 purlwise with yarn in front, K2, purl across to last 3 sts, K2, P1; turn.

Row 2: Slip 1 purlwise with yarn in back, knit across; turn.

Repeat Rows 1 and 2, 14{15} times.

HEEL TURNING

Begin working in short rows as follows:

Row 1 (Wrong side): P 17{18}, P2 tog, P1, leave remaining 10{11} sts unworked; **turn.**

Continue to slip the first stitch, holding yarn to **wrong** side, and slipping knitwise on all **right** side rows and purlwise on all **wrong** side rows.

Row 2: Slip 1, K5, SSK, K1; turn.

Row 3: Slip 1, P6, P2 tog, P1; turn.

Row 4: Slip 1, K7, SSK, K1; turn.

Row 5: Slip 1, P8, P2 tog, P1; turn.

Row 6: Slip 1, K9, SSK, K1; turn.

Row 7: Slip 1, P 10, P2 tog, P1; turn.

Row 8: Slip 1, K 11, SSK, K1; turn.

Row 9: Slip 1, P 12, P2 tog, P1; turn.

Row 10: Slip 1, K 13, SSK, K1; turn.

Row 11: Slip 1, P 14, P2 tog, P1; turn.

Row 12: Slip 1, K 15, SSK, K1; turn.

Woman's Size Only
Row 13: Slip 1, P 15, P2 tog; turn.

Row 14: Slip 1, K 14, SSK: 16 sts.

Man's Size Only
Row 13: Slip 1, P 16, P2 tog; turn.

Row 14: Slip 1, K 16, SSK: 18 sts.

GUSSET

Rnd 1: With **right** side of Heel facing and using needle holding Heel sts (Needle 1), pick up 15{16} sts along edge of Heel Flap *(Fig. 17, page 93)*, pick up one st in gap between Heel Flap and Instep, K 0{1} from Instep sts *(see Zeros, page 89)*; with empty needle, work 30{32} Instep sts in established Braided Cable pattern (Needle 2); with empty needle, K 0{1} remaining Instep st, pick up one st in gap between Instep and Heel Flap, pick up 15{16} sts along edge of Heel Flap, knit first 8{9} sts of Heel from Needle 1 (Needle 3), place marker around next st to indicate beginning of rnd: 78{86} sts, arranged 24-30-24 {27-32-27}.

Continued on page 17.

CHEVRON PURLS SOCKS

Sizes	Finished Foot Circumference		Finished Foot Length	
Woman	7"	(18 cm)	9½"	(24 cm)
Man	8"	(20.5 cm)	11"	(28 cm)

Size Note: The Woman's size can easily be made to fit children ages 10-12 by making the foot length shorter *(see Sizing, page 89)*. Instructions are written for Woman's size with Man's size in braces { }. Instructions will be easier to read if you circle all the numbers pertaining to your size. If only one number is given, it applies to both sizes.

MATERIALS
Light Weight Yarn 🧶**3**
[3.5 ounces, 306 yards
(100 grams, 280 meters) per
skein]: 1{2} skein(s)
Set of 4 double pointed knitting
   needles, size 3 (3.25 mm) **or** size
   needed for gauge
Split-ring marker
Tapestry needle

GAUGE: In Stockinette Stitch,
           14 sts and 19 rnds = 2"
           (5 cm)

✓ *Take the time to check your gauge.*

Techniques used:
• K2 tog *(Fig. 9, page 92)*
• K3 tog *(Fig. 10, page 92)*
• SSK *(Figs. 12a-c, page 92)*
• P2 tog *(Fig. 15, page 93)*

CHEVRON PURLS (multiple of 8 sts)
Rnd 1: Knit around.
Rnd 2: K3, P1, ★ K7, P1; repeat from ★ around to last 4 sts, K4.
Rnd 3: K2, P3, ★ K5, P3; repeat from ★ around to last 3 sts, K3.
Rnd 4: (K1, P2) twice, ★ K3, P2, K1, P2; repeat from ★ around to last 2 sts, K2.
Rnd 5: ★ P2, K3, P2, K1; repeat from ★ around.
Rnd 6: ★ P1, K5, P1, K1; repeat from ★ around.
Rnd 7: Knit around.
Repeat Rnds 1-7 for Chevron Purls pattern.

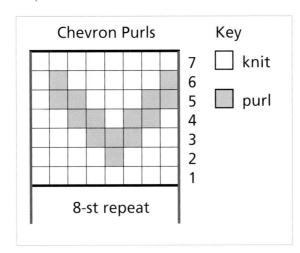

CUFF
Cast on 48{56} sts loosely.

Divide stitches onto 3 needles, arranged 16-16-16 {19-18-19}.

Place a marker around the first stitch and join for working in the round, being careful not to twist stitches *(see Double Pointed Needles, page 90)*.

Work in K1, P1 ribbing until Sock measures 1¹/₂" (4 cm) from cast on edge.

LEG
Work in Chevron Purls pattern until Sock measures 5{6}"/12.5{15} cm from cast on edge, ending by working Rnd 7.

Man's Size Only: Remove marker, using Needle 3, K1 from Needle 1 and move marker to next st on Needle 1 to change the beginning of the round: sts arranged 18-18-20.

HEEL
Dividing Row: Knit across Needle 1, with same needle, knit 8{10} sts from Needle 2; slip remaining sts from Needle 2 onto Needle 3 and leave these 24{28} sts unworked for Instep.

The Heel Flap will be worked back and forth in rows across the first 24{28} stitches.

HEEL FLAP
Row 1 (Wrong side): Slip 1 purlwise with yarn in front, purl across; turn.

Row 2: Slip 1 purlwise with yarn in back, knit across; turn.

Repeat Rows 1 and 2, 11{13} times.

HEEL TURNING
Begin working in short rows as follows:

Row 1 (Wrong side): P 14{16}, P2 tog, P1, leave remaining 7{9} sts unworked; turn.

Continuing to slip the first stitch holding yarn to wrong side, slip knitwise on all right side rows and purlwise on all wrong side rows.

Row 2: Slip 1, K5, SSK, K1; turn.

Row 3: Slip 1, P6, P2 tog, P1; turn.

Row 4: Slip 1, K7, SSK, K1; turn.

Row 5: Slip 1, P8, P2 tog, P1; turn.

Row 6: Slip 1, K9, SSK, K1; turn.

Row 7: Slip 1, P 10, P2 tog, P1; turn.

Row 8: Slip 1, K 11, SSK, K1; turn.

Woman's Size Only
Row 9: Slip 1, P 12, P2 tog; turn.

Row 10: Slip 1, K 12, SSK: 14 sts.

Man's Size Only
Row 9: Slip 1, P 12, P2 tog, P1; turn.

Row 10: Slip 1, K 13, SSK, K1; turn.

Row 11: Slip 1, P 14, P2 tog; turn.

Row 12: Slip 1, K 14, SSK: 16 sts.

GUSSET
Rnd 1: With right side of Heel facing and using needle holding Heel sts (Needle 1), pick up 12{14} sts along edge of Heel Flap *(Fig. 17, page 93)*; with empty needle, pick up 1{0} st(s) in gap between Heel Flap and Instep *(see Zeros, page 89)*, K 0{3} Instep sts, work in established Chevron Purls pattern across next 24 Instep sts, K 0{1}, pick up 0{1} st(s) in gap between Heel Flap and Instep (Needle 2); with empty needle, pick up 12{14} sts along edge of Heel Flap, knit first 7{8} sts of Heel from Needle 1 (Needle 3), place marker around next st to indicate beginning of rnd: 63{73} sts, arranged 19-25-19 {22-29-22}.

Rnd 2 (Decrease rnd): On Needle 1, knit across needle to last 3 sts, K2 tog, K1; on Needle 2, work across in established Chevron Purls pattern; on Needle 3, K1, SSK, knit across: 61{71} sts.

CHEVRON PURLS SOCKS
continued from page 15.

Rnd 3: On Needle 1, knit across; on Needle 2, work across in established Chevron Purls pattern; on Needle 3, knit across.

Repeat Rnds 2 and 3, 5{6} times: 51{59} sts, arranged 13-25-13 {15-29-15}.

Woman's Size Only - Next Rnd: On Needle 1, knit across needle to last 4 sts, K3 tog, K1; on Needle 2, work across in established Chevron Purls pattern; on Needle 3, K1, SSK, knit across. Slip first st from Needle 2 onto Needle 1: 48 sts, arranged 12-24-12.

Man's Size Only - Next Rnd: On Needle 1, knit across needle to last 3 sts, K2 tog, K1; on Needle 2, work across in established Chevron Purls pattern; on Needle 3, K1, separately slip 3 sts knitwise, insert the left hand needle into the front of all 3 slipped sts and knit them together, knit across. Slip last st from Needle 2 onto Needle 3: 56 sts, arranged 14-28-14.

FOOT

Work in Chevron Purls pattern on all stitches until Foot measures approximately 8{9}"/20.5{23} cm from back of Heel, **or** about 1½{2}"/4{5} cm shorter than desired length of Sock.

TOE

Rnd 1 (Decrease rnd): On Needle 1, knit across needle to last 3 sts, K2 tog, K1; on Needle 2, K1, SSK, knit across needle to last 3 sts, K2 tog, K1; on Needle 3, K1, SSK, knit across: 44{52} sts.

Rnd 2: Knit around.

Repeat Rnds 1 and 2, 6{7} times: 20{24} sts.

Repeat Rnd 1 only, 2{3} times: 12 sts.

FINISHING

With Needle 3, knit sts from Needle 1: 6 sts on both needles.

With tapestry needle, graft Toe *(Figs. 18a & b, page 94)*.
Weave in ends.

BRIGHT TWEED SOCKS
continued from page 7.

FOOT

Knit each round until Foot measures approximately 8" (20.5 cm) from back of Heel, **or** about 1½" (4 cm) shorter than desired length of Sock.

TOE

Rnd 1 (Decrease rnd): On Needle 1, knit across needle to last 3 sts, K2 tog, K1; on Needle 2, K1, SSK, knit across needle to last 3 sts, K2 tog, K1; on Needle 3, K1, SSK, knit across: 52 sts.

Rnd 2: Knit around.

Repeat Rnds 1 and 2, 6 times: 28 sts.

Repeat Rnd 1 only, 4 times: 12 sts.

FINISHING

With Needle 3, knit sts from Needle 1: 6 sts on each needle.

With tapestry needle, graft Toe *(Figs. 18a & b, page 94)*. Weave in ends.

BRAIDED CABLE SOCKS
conitnued from page 11.

Rnd 2 (Decrease rnd): On Needle 1, knit across needle to last 3 sts, K2 tog, K1; on Needle 2, work across in established Braided Cable pattern; on Needle 3, K1, SSK, knit across: 76{84} sts.

Rnd 3: On Needle 1, knit across; on Needle 2, work across in established Braided Cable pattern; on Needle 3, knit across.

Repeat Rnds 2 and 3, 8{9} times: 60{66} sts, arranged 15-30-15 {17-32-17}.

FOOT

Work even (Rnd 3 of Gusset) until Foot measures approximately 7½ {9}"/19{23} cm from back of Heel, or about 2" (5 cm) shorter than desired length of Sock.

TOE

Rnd 1 (Decrease rnd): On Needle 1, knit across needle to last 3 sts, K2 tog, K1; on Needle 2, K1, SSK, knit across needle to last 3 sts, K2 tog, K1; on Needle 3, K1, SSK, knit across: 56{62} sts.

Rnd 2: Knit around.

Repeat Rnds 1 and 2, 6{7} times: 32{34} sts.

Repeat Rnd 1 only, 5 times: 12{14} sts.

FINISHING

With Needle 3, knit 3 sts from Needle 1, transfer 0{1} st(s) to Needle 2: 6{7} sts on each needle.

With tapestry needle, graft Toe *(Figs. 18a & b, page 94)*. Weave in ends.

HEART TOE-UP SOCKS

Size: Woman
Finished Foot Circumference: 7½" (19 cm)
Finished Foot Length: 9½" (24 cm)

Size Note: These socks can easily be made to fit children ages 10-12 by making the foot length shorter *(see Sizing, page 89).*

MATERIALS

Super Fine Weight Yarn SUPER FINE [1]
[1.75 ounces, 175 yards (50 grams, 160 meters) per hank]: 2 hanks
Set of 5 double pointed knitting needles, size 2 (2.75 mm) **or** size needed for gauge
Split-ring marker
Tapestry needle

GAUGE: In Stockinette Stitch, 16 sts and 24 rnds = 2" (5 cm)

✓ *Take the time to check your gauge.*

Techniques used:

- YO *(Fig. 4, page 91)*
- M1 *(Figs. 5a & b, page 91)*
- M1-R *(Figs. 6a & b, page 91)*
- K2 tog *(Fig. 9, page 92)*
- K4 tog *(Fig. 11, page 92)*
- SSK *(Figs. 12a-c, page 92)*
- Slip 1 as if to **knit**, K2 tog, PSSO *(Fig. 14, page 93)*
- P2 tog *(Fig. 15, page 93)*

TOE

Holding two needles parallel, place a slip knot on the bottom needle to temporarily anchor the yarn. Bring the yarn behind and over the top needle, then behind and over the bottom needle. Continue in this manner *(Fig. A)* until there are 8 loops on each needle, not including the slip knot.

Fig. A

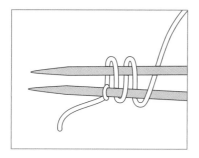

With an empty needle, K8 from the top needle. Rotate the needles so that the bottom needle is now on top, then remove the slip knot. With an empty needle, K8 from this needle: 8 sts on each needle.

Divide stitches evenly onto 4 needles, placing 4 sts on each needle *(Fig. 2c, page 90)*.

Place a marker around the first stitch to indicate the beginning of the round.

To work Right Lifted increase, insert right hand needle from the **front** into right leg of stitch **below** next stitch on left hand needle and knit this stitch *(Fig. 7, page 91)*.

To work Left Lifted increase, insert left hand needle from the **back** into left leg of stitch 2 rows **below** last st on right hand needle, pull it up and knit into the back loop of this stitch *(Figs. 8a & b, page 92)*.

Rnd 1: Knit around.

Rnd 2 (Increase rnd): ★ K1, Right Lifted increase, knit across needle; on next needle, knit across to last st, Left Lifted increase, K1; repeat from ★ once **more**: 20 sts.

Repeat Rnds 1 and 2, 10 times: 60 sts.

FOOT

Knit each round until Sock measures approximately 6¼" (16 cm) from tip of Toe, **or** about 3¼" (8.5 cm) less than desired Foot length.

GUSSET

Rnd 1 (Increase rnd): On Needles 1 and 2, knit across; on Needle 3, K1, M1-R, knit across needle; on Needle 4, knit across to last st, M1, K1: 62 sts.

Rnd 2: Knit around.

Repeat Rnds 1 and 2, 9 times; then repeat Rnd 1 once **more**: 82 sts.

HEEL

To Wrap and turn *(abbreviated w&t)*, **when last st worked is a knit st:** Slip next st purlwise with yarn in back, leave remaining sts unworked, move yarn between needles to the **front**, slip same st back to left hand needle. Turn work, moving yarn between needles to front if necessary to work the next st.
when last st worked is a purl st: Slip next st purlwise with yarn in front, leave remaining sts unworked, move yarn between needles to the **back**, slip same st back to left hand needle. Turn work, moving yarn between needles to back if necessary to work the next st.

HEEL TURNING

To work Kfb increase, knit into front **and** back of next stitch.

To work Pfb increase, purl into front **and** back of next stitch.

Work across Instep stitches (Needles 1 and 2) to Heel, then work in short rows across Heel stitches only (Needles 3 and 4) as follows:

Row 1 (Right side): Knit across first 3 needles; on Needle 4, K9, Kfb, K1, w&t.

Row 2: P 21, Pfb, P1, w&t.

Row 3: K 19, Kfb, K1, w&t.

Row 4: P 17, Pfb, P1, w&t.

Row 5: K 15, Kfb, K1, w&t.

Row 6: P 13, Pfb, P1, w&t.

Row 7: K 11, Kfb, K1, w&t.

Row 8: P9, Pfb, P1, w&t: 60 sts on Needles 3 and 4.

To knit a wrapped stitch, insert right hand needle into the wrapped stitch from **below** the wrap lying at the base of the wrapped stitch, then knit the wrap and the stitch together *(Fig. B)*.

Fig. B

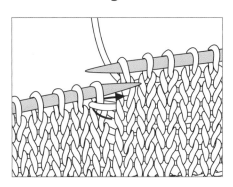

Joining Rnd: On Needle 3, K6, M1; on Needle 4, knit across knitting each wrapped st as you come to it; on Needles 1 and 2, knit across Instep sts: 91 sts.

HEEL FLAP

The Heel Flap will be worked back and forth in rows across Needles 3 and 4 only.

Row 1 (Right side): Knit across 45 sts knitting each wrapped st as you come to it, SSK; turn.

When instructed to slip a stitch, slip 1 purlwise with yarn in back, unless otherwise specified.

Row 2: Slip 1, P 29, P2 tog; turn.

Row 3: (Slip 1, K1) 15 times, SSK; turn.

Rows 4-30: Repeat Rows 2 and 3, 13 times; then repeat Row 2 once **more**: 31 sts.

Row 31: K 14, K2 tog, knit across: 30 sts.

LEG

Working in the round on all 60 stitches, knit each round until Leg measures approximately 4" (10 cm) from bottom of Heel.

HEART LACE PATTERN

Rnd 1: ★ K1, YO, K2 tog, K3, YO, K1, YO, K3, SSK, YO; repeat from ★ around: 70 sts.

Rnd 2: Knit around.

To work SSSSK (*slip, slip, slip, slip, knit*; uses 4 sts), separately slip next 4 sts knitwise, insert left hand needle into front of all 4 slipped sts and knit them together as if they were one st.

Rnd 3: K2, YO, K4 tog, YO, K3, YO, SSSSK, YO, ★ K3, YO, K4 tog, YO, K3, YO, SSSSK, YO; repeat from ★ around to last st, K1: 60 sts.

Rnd 4: Knit around.

Rnd 5: K2, K2 tog, YO, K5, YO, SSK, ★ K3, K2 tog, YO, K5, YO, SSK; repeat from ★ around to last st, K1.

Rnd 6: Knit around.

Rnd 7: ★ K1, K2 tog, YO, K7, YO, SSK; repeat from ★ around.

Rnd 8: Knit around.

Rnd 9: ★ YO, slip 1, K2 tog, PSSO, YO, K9; repeat from ★ around.

Rnd 10: Knit around.

Rnd 11: ★ K1, YO, K2 tog, K3, YO, K1, YO, K3, SSK, YO; repeat from ★ around: 70 sts.

Rnd 12: Knit around.

Rnd 13: K2, YO, K4 tog, YO, K3, YO, SSSSK, YO, ★ K3, YO, K4 tog, YO, K3, YO, SSSSK, YO; repeat from ★ around to last st, K1: 60 sts.

Rnds 14-16: Knit around.

CUFF

Work in K1, P1 ribbing for 1¼" (3 cm).

Bind off loosely in ribbing using a tapestry needle bind off if desired *(Fig. 16, page 93)*. Weave in ends.

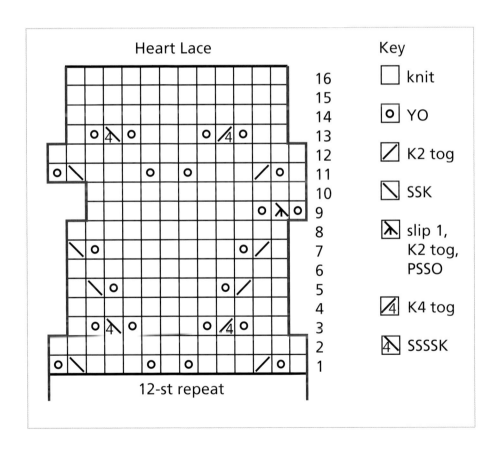

Heart Lace

Key

☐ knit

⊙ YO

⧄ K2 tog

⧅ SSK

⋀ slip 1, K2 tog, PSSO

4 K4 tog

SSSSK

12-st repeat

EYELET TOE-UP SOCKS

■■■□ INTERMEDIATE

Size: Woman
Finished Foot Circumference: 7¹/₂" (19 cm)
Finished Foot Length: 9¹/₂" (24 cm)

Size Note: These socks can easily be made to fit children ages 10-12 by making the foot length shorter *(see Sizing, page 89)*.

MATERIALS

SUPER FINE **1**

Super Fine Weight Yarn
[1.75 ounces, 175 yards
(50 grams, 160 meters) per hank]:
  2 hanks
Set of 5 double pointed knitting
  needles, size 2 (2.75 mm) **or** size
  needed for gauge
Split-ring marker
Tapestry needle

GAUGE: In Stockinette Stitch,
  16 sts and 24 rnds =
  2" (5 cm)

✓ *Take the time to check your gauge.*

Techniques used:
• YO *(Fig. 4, page 91)*
• M1 *(Figs. 5a & b, page 91)*
• M1-R *(Figs. 6a & b, page 91)*
• K2 tog *(Fig. 9, page 92)*
• SSK *(Figs. 12a-c, page 92)*
• P2 tog *(Fig. 15, page 93)*

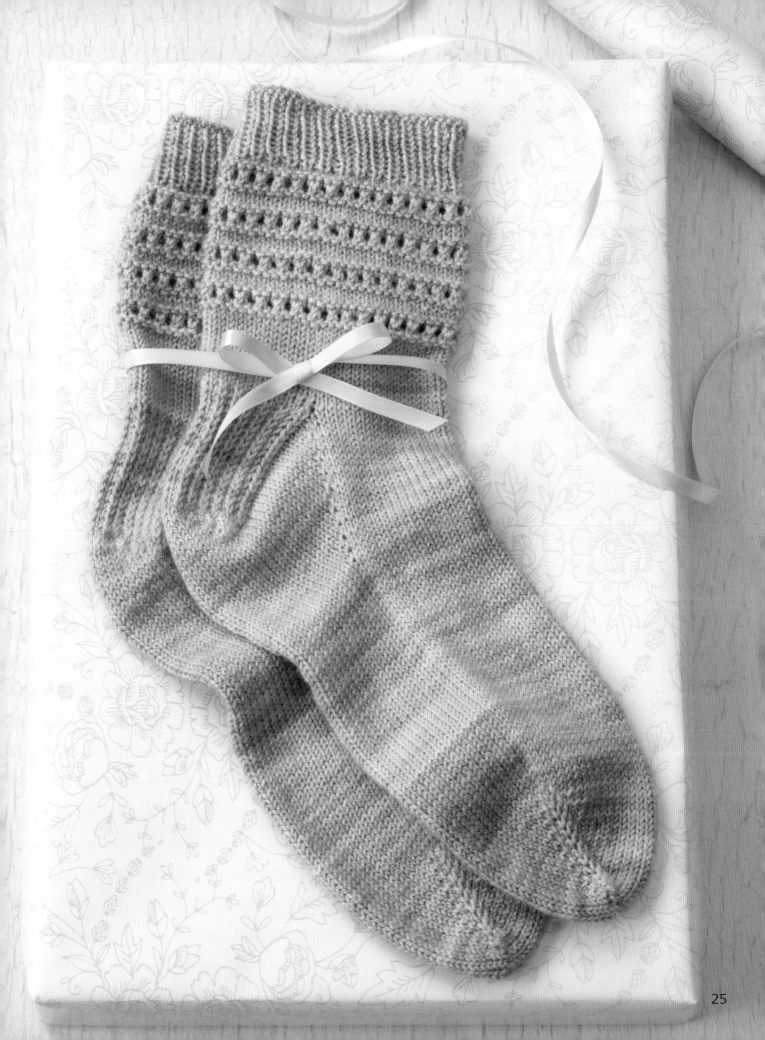

TOE

Holding two needles parallel, place a slip knot on the bottom needle to temporarily anchor the yarn. Bring the yarn behind and over the top needle, then behind and over the bottom needle. Continue in this manner *(Fig. C)* until there are 8 loops on each needle, not including the slip knot.

Fig. C

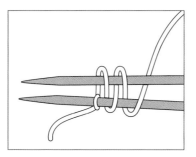

With an empty needle, K8 from the top needle. Rotate the needles so that the bottom needle is now on top, then remove the slip knot. With an empty needle, K8 from this needle: 8 sts on each needle.

Divide stitches evenly onto 4 needles, placing 4 sts on each needle *(Fig. 2c, page 90)*.

Place a marker around the first stitch to indicate the beginning of the round.

To work **Right Lifted increase**, insert right hand needle from the **front** into right leg of stitch **below** next stitch on left hand needle and knit this stitch *(Fig. 7, page 91)*.

To work **Left Lifted increase**, insert left hand needle from the **back** into left leg of stitch 2 rows **below** last st on right hand needle, pull it up and knit into the back loop of this stitch *(Figs. 8a & b, page 92)*.

Rnd 1: Knit around.

Rnd 2 (Increase rnd): ★ K1, Right Lifted increase, knit across needle; on next needle, knit across to last st, Left Lifted increase, K1; repeat from ★ once **more**: 20 sts.

Repeat Rnds 1 and 2, 10 times: 60 sts.

FOOT

Knit each round until Sock measures approximately 6¼" (16 cm) from tip of Toe, **or** about 3¼" (8.5 cm) less than desired Foot length.

GUSSET

Rnd 1 (Increase rnd): On Needles 1 and 2, knit across; on Needle 3, K1, M1-R, knit across needle; on Needle 4, knit across to last st, M1, K1: 62 sts.

Rnd 2: Knit around.

Repeat Rnds 1 and 2, 9 times; then repeat Rnd 1 once **more**: 82 sts.

HEEL
To Wrap and turn *(abbreviated w&t),*
when last st worked is a knit st: Slip next st purlwise with yarn in back, leave remaining sts unworked, move yarn between needles to the **front**, slip same st back to left hand needle. Turn work, moving yarn between needles to front if necessary to work the next st.
when last st worked is a purl st: Slip next st purlwise with yarn in front, leave remaining sts unworked, move yarn between needles to the **back**, slip same st back to left hand needle. Turn work, moving yarn between needles to back if necessary to work the next st.

HEEL TURNING
To work Kfb increase, knit into front **and** back of next stitch.

To work Pfb increase, purl into front **and** back of next stitch.

Work across Instep stitches (Needles 1 and 2) to Heel, then work in short rows across Heel stitches only (Needles 3 and 4) as follows:

Row 1 (Right side): Knit across first 3 needles; on Needle 4, K9, Kfb, K1, w&t.

Row 2: P 21, Pfb, P1, w&t.

Row 3: K 19, Kfb, K1, w&t.

Row 4: P 17, Pfb, P1, w&t.

Row 5: K 15, Kfb, K1, w&t.

Row 6: P 13, Pfb, P1, w&t.

Row 7: K 11, Kfb, K1, w&t.

Row 8: P9, Pfb, P1, w&t: 60 sts on Needles 3 and 4.

To knit a wrapped stitch, insert right hand needle into the wrapped stitch from **below** the wrap lying at the base of the wrapped stitch, then knit the wrap and the stitch together *(Fig. B, page 21).*

Joining Rnd: On Needle 3, K6, M1; on Needle 4, knit across knitting each wrapped st as you come to it; on Needles 1 and 2, knit across Instep sts: 91 sts.

HEEL FLAP
The Heel Flap will be worked back and forth in rows across Needles 3 and 4 only.

Row 1 (Right side): Knit across 45 sts knitting each wrapped st as you come to it, SSK; turn.

When instructed to slip a stitch, slip 1 purlwise with yarn in back unless otherwise specified.

Row 2: Slip 1, P 29, P2 tog; turn.

Row 3: (Slip 1, K1) 15 times, SSK; turn.

Rows 4-30: Repeat Rows 2 and 3, 13 times; then repeat Row 2 once **more**: 31 sts.

Row 31: K 14, K2 tog, knit across: 30 sts.

Continued on page 40.

KNOTTED RIB SOCKS

Size: Man
Finished Foot Circumference: 8 " (20.5 cm)
Finished Foot Length: 11 " (28 cm)

Size Note: These socks can easily be made to fit a woman by making the foot length shorter *(see Sizing, page 89)*.

MATERIALS

SUPER FINE **❶**

Super Fine Weight Yarn
[3.5 ounces, 436 yards
(100 grams, 398 meters) per skein]:
  1 skein
Set of 4 double pointed knitting
  needles, size 2 (2.75 mm) **or** size
  needed for gauge
Split-ring marker
Tapestry needle

GAUGE: In Stockinette Stitch,
16 sts and 20 rnds =
2 " (5 cm)

✔ *Take the time to check your gauge.*

Techniques used:
- K2 tog *(Fig. 9, page 92)*
- K3 tog *(Fig. 10, page 92)*
- SSK *(Figs. 12a-c, page 92)*
- P2 tog *(Fig. 15, page 93)*

LEG

Cast on 64 sts loosely.

Divide stitches onto 3 needles, arranged 21-22-21.

Place a marker around the first stitch and join for working in the round, being careful not to twist stitches *(see Double Pointed Needles, page 90)*.

Rnds 1-4: ★ P1, K1; repeat from ★ around.

Rnd 5: ★ P1, knit into the front, back, **and** front of next st, P1, K1; repeat from ★ around: 96 sts.

Rnd 6: ★ P1, K3 tog, P1, K1; repeat from ★ around: 64 sts.

Rnds 7-12: ★ P1, K1; repeat from ★ around.

Repeat Rnds 5-12 for Knotted Rib pattern until Sock measures approximately 7" (18 cm) from cast on edge, ending by working Rnd 12.

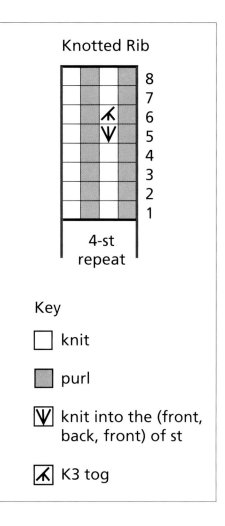

Knotted Rib

				8
				7
	⋏			6
	V			5
				4
				3
				2
				1

4-st repeat

Key

□ knit

▨ purl

|V| knit into the (front, back, front) of st

|⋏| K3 tog

HEEL

Dividing Row: Knit across Needle 1, with same needle, knit 11 sts from Needle 2; slip remaining sts from Needle 2 onto Needle 3 and leave these 32 sts unworked for Instep.

The Heel Flap will be worked back and forth in rows across the first 32 stitches.

HEEL FLAP

Row 1 (Wrong side): Slip 1 purlwise with yarn in front, purl across; turn.

Row 2: Slip 1 purlwise with yarn in back, knit across; turn.

Repeat Rows 1 and 2, 15 times.

HEEL TURNING

Begin working in short rows as follows:

Row 1 (Wrong side): P 18, P2 tog, P1, leave remaining 11 sts unworked; **turn.**

Continuing to slip the first stitch holding yarn to **wrong** side, slip knitwise on all **right** side rows and purlwise on all **wrong** side rows.

Row 2: Slip 1, K5, SSK, K1; turn.

Row 3: Slip 1, P6, P2 tog, P1; turn.

Row 4: Slip 1, K7, SSK, K1; turn.

Row 5: Slip 1, P8, P2 tog, P1; turn.

Row 6: Slip 1, K9, SSK, K1; turn.

Row 7: Slip 1, P 10, P2 tog, P1; turn.

Row 8: Slip 1, K 11, SSK, K1; turn.

Row 9: Slip 1, P 12, P2 tog, P1; turn.

Row 10: Slip 1, K 13, SSK, K1; turn.

Row 11: Slip 1, P 14, P2 tog, P1; turn.

Row 12: Slip 1, K 15, SSK, K1; turn.

Row 13: Slip 1, P 16, P2 tog; turn.

Row 14: Slip 1, K 16, SSK: 18 sts.

GUSSET

Rnd 1: With **right** side of Heel facing and using needle holding Heel sts (Needle 1), pick up 16 sts along edge of Heel Flap *(Fig. 17, page 93)*; with empty needle, pick up one st in gap between Heel Flap and Instep, (P1, K1) across (Needle 2); with empty needle, pick up one st in gap between Instep and Heel Flap, pick up 16 sts along edge of Heel Flap, knit first 9 sts of Heel from Needle 1 (Needle 3), place marker around next st to indicate beginning of rnd: 84 sts, arranged 25-33-26.

Rnd 2 (Decrease rnd): On Needle 1, knit across needle to last 3 sts, K2 tog, K1; on Needle 2, K1, (P1, K1) across; on Needle 3, K1, SSK, knit across: 82 sts.

Rnd 3: On Needle 1, knit across; on Needle 2, K1, (P1, K1) across; on Needle 3, knit across.

Repeat Rnds 2 and 3, 9 times: 64 sts.

Slip first stitch from Needle 2 onto Needle 1: 64 sts, arranged 16-32-16.

Continued on page 41.

SEED STRIPES SOCKS

Sizes	Finished Foot Circumference	Finished Foot Length
Woman	7" (18 cm)	9½" (24 cm)
Man	8" (20.5 cm)	11" (28 cm)

Size Note: The Woman's size can easily be made to fit children ages 10-12 by making the foot length shorter *(see Sizing, page 89)*. Instructions are written for Woman's size with Man's size in braces { }. Instructions will be easier to read if you circle all the numbers pertaining to your size. If only one number is given, it applies to both sizes.

MATERIALS

SUPER FINE 1

Super Fine Weight Yarn
[3.5 ounces, 436 yards
(100 grams, 400 meters) per ball]:
  1 ball
Set of 4 double pointed knitting
  needles, size 1 (2.25 mm) **or** size
  needed for gauge
Split-ring marker
Tapestry needle

GAUGE: In Stockinette Stitch,
  16 sts and 20 rnds =
  2" (5 cm)
✓ *Take the time to check your gauge.*

Techniques used:
- K2 tog *(Fig. 9, page 92)*
- SSK *(Figs. 12a-c, page 92)*
- P2 tog *(Fig. 15, page 93)*

CUFF

Cast on 56{64} sts loosely.

Divide stitches onto 3 needles, arranged 19-18-19 {21-22-21}.

Place a marker around the first stitch and join for working in the round, being careful not to twist stitches *(see Double Pointed Needles, page 90)*.

Work in K1, P1 ribbing until Sock measures 1¹/₂" (4 cm) from cast on edge.

LEG

Rnds 1-4: Knit around.

Rnd 5: ★ K1, P1; repeat from ★ around.

Rnd 6: ★ P1, K1; repeat from ★ around.

Rnds 7-12: Repeat Rnds 5 and 6, 3 times.

Rnds 13-16: Knit around.

Rnds 17-20: Repeat Rnds 5 and 6 twice.

Repeat Rnds 13-20 for Seed Stripes pattern, 2{3} times.

HEEL

Dividing Row: On Needle 1, K1, (P1, K1) across needle, continuing with same needle, P1, (K1, P1) 4{5} times across Needle 2; slip remaining sts from Needle 2 onto Needle 3 and leave these 28{32} sts unworked for Instep.

The Heel Flap will be worked back and forth in rows across the first 28{32} stitches.

HEEL FLAP

Row 1 (Wrong side): Slip 1 purlwise with yarn in front, K1, ★ P1, K1; repeat from ★ across to last 2 sts, P2; turn.

Row 2: Slip 1 purlwise with yarn in back, P1, ★ K1, P1; repeat from ★ across to last 2 sts, K2; turn.

Repeat Rows 1 and 2, 13{15} times.

HEEL TURNING

Begin working in short rows as follows:

Row 1 (Wrong side): P 16{18}, P2 tog, P1, leave remaining 9{11} sts unworked; turn.

Continuing to slip the first stitch holding yarn to **wrong** side, slip knitwise on all **right** side rows and purlwise on all **wrong** side rows.

Row 2: Slip 1, K5, SSK, K1; turn.

Row 3: Slip 1, P6, P2 tog, P1; turn.

Row 4: Slip 1, K7, SSK, K1; turn.

Row 5: Slip 1, P8, P2 tog, P1; turn.

Row 6: Slip 1, K9, SSK, K1; turn.

Row 7: Slip 1, P 10, P2 tog, P1; turn.

Row 8: Slip 1, K 11, SSK, K1; turn.

Row 9: Slip 1, P 12, P2 tog, P1; turn.

Row 10: Slip 1, K 13, SSK, K1; turn.

Woman's Size Only
Row 11: Slip 1, P 14, P2 tog; turn.

Row 12: Slip 1, K 14, SSK: 16 sts.

Man's Size Only
Row 11: Slip 1, P 14, P2 tog, P1; turn.

Row 12: Slip 1, K 15, SSK, K1; turn.

Row 13: Slip 1, P 16, P2 tog; turn.

Row 14: Slip 1, K 16, SSK: 18 sts.

GUSSET

Continue Seed Stripes pattern on Instep stitches (alternating 4 knit rounds and 4 Seed Stitch rounds).

To maintain Seed Stitch, knit the purl stitches and purl the knit stitches as they face you.

Rnd 1: With **right** side of Heel facing and using needle holding Heel sts (Needle 1), pick up 14{16} sts along edge of Heel Flap *(Fig. 17, page 93)*, pick up one st in gap between Heel Flap and Instep; with empty needle, knit 28{32} Instep sts (Needle 2); with empty needle, pick up one st in gap between Instep and Heel Flap, pick up 14{16} sts along edge of Heel Flap, knit first 8{9} sts of Heel from Needle 1 (Needle 3), place marker around next st to indicate beginning of rnd: 74{84} sts, arranged 23-28-23 {26-32-26}.

Rnd 2 (Decrease rnd): On Needle 1, knit across needle to last 3 sts, K2 tog, K1; on Needle 2, work across in established Seed Stripes pattern; on Needle 3, K1, SSK, knit across: 72{82} sts.

Rnd 3: On Needle 1, knit across; on Needle 2, work across in established Seed Stripes pattern; on Needle 3, knit across.

Repeat Rnds 2 and 3, 8{9} times: 56{64} sts, arranged 14-28-14 {16-32-16}.

FOOT

Work even (Rnd 3 of Gusset) until Foot measures approximately 7½{9}"/19{23} cm from back of Heel, **or** about 2" (5 cm) shorter than desired length of Sock.

Continued on page 41.

TWO-RIBBED SOCKS

■■■□ INTERMEDIATE

Size: Woman
Finished Foot Circumference: 7" (18 cm)
Finished Foot Length: 9" (23 cm)

Size Note: These socks can easily be made to fit children ages 10-12 by making the foot length shorter *(see Sizing, page 89)*.

MATERIALS
Super Fine Weight Yarn **SUPER FINE 1**
[3.5 ounces, 438 yards
(100 grams, 400 meters) per skein]:
  1 skein
Set of 4 double pointed knitting
  needles, size 2 (2.75 mm) **or** size
  needed for gauge
Split-ring marker
Stitch holder
Tapestry needle

GAUGE: In Stockinette Stitch,
  16 sts and 20 rnds =
  2" (5 cm)
✓ *Take the time to check
  your gauge.*

Techniques used:
- tbl *(Fig. 3, page 91)*
- K2 tog *(Fig. 9, page 92)*
- K3 tog *(Fig. 10, page 92)*
- SSK *(Figs. 12a-c, page 92)*
- P2 tog *(Fig. 15, page 93)*

Cuff is worked back-and-forth from side to side, then Leg stitches are picked up and worked in the round.

CUFF
Cast on 16 sts loosely.

Row 1: Slip 1 purlwise with yarn in front, ★ K1-tbl, P1; repeat from ★ across to last st, K1.

Repeat Row 1 until Cuff measures approximately 8" (20.5 cm) from cast on edge, ending by working a **wrong** side row.

To work bind off, fold Cuff so that cast on edge is parallel to and behind sts on needle. Insert right hand needle into next st on needle **and** into first cast on st and knit these 2 sts together; ★ knit together next pair of sts, bind off one st; repeat from ★ until all sts have been bound off. Finish off last st.

LEG
Turn Cuff right side out (with seam on inside). With **right** side facing and beginning at seam, pick up 56 sts evenly spaced around onto 3 needles *(Fig. 17, page 93)*, arranged 19-18-19; place a marker around the first st to indicate beginning of rnd.

PATTERN: K7, † (P1, K1-tbl) 3 times, P2, (K1-tbl, P1) 3 times †, K 14, repeat from † to † once, K7.

Work in Pattern until Sock measures approximately 5½" (14 cm) from cast on edge.

HEEL
Dividing Row: Work across 14 sts in pattern, slip next 28 sts onto st holder for Instep.

The Heel Flap will be worked back and forth in rows across the remaining 28 stitches, combining all stitches onto one needle.

HEEL FLAP
Row 1 (Wrong side)**:** Slip 1 knitwise with yarn in back, (P1-tbl, K1) 3 times, P 14, (K1, P1-tbl) 3 times, K1; turn.

Row 2: Slip 1 purlwise with yarn in front, (K1-tbl, P1) 3 times, K 14, (P1, K1-tbl) 3 times, P1; turn.

Repeat Rows 1 and 2, 13 times.

HEEL TURNING

Begin working in short rows as follows:

Row 1 (Wrong side): P 16, P2 tog, P1, leave remaining 9 sts unworked; **turn**.

Slip the first stitch holding yarn to **wrong** side, slip knitwise on all **right** side rows and purlwise on all **wrong** side rows.

Row 2: Slip 1, K5, SSK, K1; turn.

Row 3: Slip 1, P6, P2 tog, P1; turn.

Row 4: Slip 1, K7, SSK, K1; turn.

Row 5: Slip 1, P8, P2 tog, P1; turn.

Row 6: Slip 1, K9, SSK, K1; turn.

Row 7: Slip 1, P 10, P2 tog, P1; turn.

Row 8: Slip 1, K 11, SSK, K1; turn.

Row 9: Slip 1, P 12, P2 tog, P1; turn.

Row 10: Slip 1, K 13, SSK, K1; turn.

Row 11: Slip 1, P 14, P2 tog; turn.

Row 12: Slip 1, K 14, SSK: 16 sts.

GUSSET

Rnd 1: With **right** side of Heel facing and using needle holding Heel sts (Needle 1), pick up 14 sts along edge of Heel Flap, pick up one st in gap between Heel Flap and Instep; slip 28 Instep sts onto empty needle, with empty needle, P1, (K1-tbl, P1) 3 times, K 14, P1, (K1-tbl, P1) 3 times (Needle 2); with empty needle, pick up one st in gap between Instep and Heel Flap, pick up 14 sts along edge of Heel Flap, knit first 8 sts of Heel from Needle 1 (Needle 3), place marker around next st to indicate beginning of rnd: 74 sts, arranged 23-28-23.

Rnd 2 (Decrease rnd): On Needle 1, knit across needle to last 3 sts, K2 tog, K1; on Needle 2, work across in established pattern; on Needle 3, K1, SSK, knit across: 72 sts.

Rnd 3: On Needle 1, knit across; on Needle 2, work across in established pattern; on Needle 3, knit across.

Repeat Rnds 2 and 3, 8 times: 56 sts, arranged 14-28-14.

FOOT

Work even (Rnd 3 of Gusset) until Foot measures approximately 7½" (19 cm) from back of Heel, **or** about 1½" (4 cm) shorter than desired length of Sock.

TOE

Rnd 1 (Decrease rnd): On Needle 1, knit across needle to last 3 sts, K2 tog, K1; on Needle 2, P1, (K1-tbl, P1) 3 times, SSK, knit across needle to last 9 sts, K2 tog, P1, (K1-tbl, P1) 3 times; on Needle 3, K1, SSK, knit across: 52 sts.

Rnd 2: On Needle 1, knit across; on Needle 2, work across in established pattern; on Needle 3, knit across.

Rnds 3-12: Repeat Rnds 1 and 2, 5 times: 32 sts.

TWO-RIBBED SOCKS continued from page 39.

To work s2kp (uses 3 sts), slip 2 together knitwise, K1, pass 2 slipped sts over knit st.

To work SSSK *(slip, slip, slip, knit*; uses 3 sts*)*, separately slip next 3 sts knitwise, insert left hand needle into all 3 sts and knit them together as if they were one st.

Rnd 13: On Needle 1, K4, K3 tog, K1; on Needle 2, s2kp, (K1-tbl, P1) twice, K2, (P1, K1-tbl) twice, s2kp; on Needle 3, K1, SSSK, K4: 24 sts.

Rnd 14: On Needle 1, K2, K3 tog, K1; on Needle 2, s2kp, K1-tbl, P1, K2, P1, K1-tbl, s2kp; on Needle 3, K1, SSSK, K2: 16 sts.

FINISHING
With Needle 3, knit sts from Needle 1: 8 sts on both needles.

With tapestry needle, graft Toe *(Figs. 18a & b, page 94).* Weave in ends.

EYELET TOE-UP SOCKS continued from page 27.

LEG
Working in the round on all 60 stitches, knit each round until Leg measures approximately 4" (10 cm) from bottom of Heel.

EYELET RIDGE PATTERN
Rnd 1: Knit around.

Rnd 2: Purl around.

Rnd 3: Knit around.

Rnd 4: ★ YO, K2 tog; repeat from ★ around.

Rnd 5: Knit around.

Rnd 6: Purl around.

Rnds 7-9: Knit around.

Repeat Rnds 2-9 twice for Eyelet Ridge pattern, then repeat Rnds 2-8 once **more**.

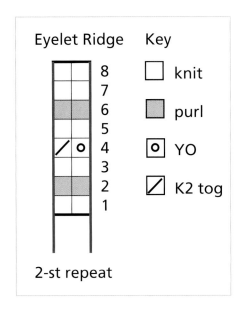

Eyelet Ridge

	8
	7
	6
	5
	4
	3
	2
	1

2-st repeat

Key

☐ knit

▨ purl

◉ YO

◪ K2 tog

CUFF

Work in K1, P1 ribbing for 1¼" (3 cm).

Bind off loosely in ribbing using the tapestry needle bind off if desired *(Fig. 16, page 93)*. Weave in ends.

KNOTTED RIB SOCKS continued from page 31.

FOOT

Work even (Rnd 3 of Gusset) until Foot measures approximately 9" (23 cm) from back of Heel, **or** about 2" (5 cm) shorter than desired length of Sock.

TOE

Rnd 1 (Decrease rnd): On Needle 1, knit across needle to last 3 sts, K2 tog, K1; on Needle 2, K1, SSK, knit across needle to last 3 sts, K2 tog, K1; on Needle 3, K1, SSK, knit across: 60 sts.

Rnd 2: Knit around.

Repeat Rnds 1 and 2, 7 times: 32 sts.

Repeat Rnd 1 only, 5 times: 12 sts.

FINISHING

With Needle 3, knit sts from Needle 1: 6 sts on both needles.

With tapestry needle, graft Toe *(Figs. 18a & b, page 94)*. Weave in ends.

SEED STRIPES SOCKS continued from page 35.

TOE

Rnd 1 (Decrease rnd): On Needle 1, knit across needle to last 3 sts, K2 tog, K1; on Needle 2, K1, SSK, knit across needle to last 3 sts, K2 tog, K1; on Needle 3, K1, SSK, knit across: 52{60} sts.

Rnd 2: Knit around.

Repeat Rnds 1 and 2, 6{7} times: 28{32} sts.

Repeat Rnd 1 only, 4{5} times: 12 sts.

FINISHING

With Needle 3, knit sts from Needle 1: 6 sts on both needles.

With tapestry needle, graft Toe *(Figs. 18a & b, page 94)*. Weave in ends.

TINY TOES SOCKS

◖■■◻ INTERMEDIATE

Baby Sizes	Finished Foot Circumference	Finished Foot Length
3-6 months	4" (10 cm)	3½" (9 cm)
6-12 months	4" (10 cm)	3¾" (9.5 cm)
18-24 months	4½" (11.5 cm)	4½" (11.5 cm)

Size Note: Instructions are written for size 3-6 months with sizes 6-12 months and 18-24 months in braces { }. Instructions will be easier to read if you circle all the numbers pertaining to your size. If only one number is given, it applies to all sizes.

MATERIALS

Super Fine Weight Yarn **SUPER FINE 1**
[1.75 ounces, 177 yards (50 grams, 162 meters) per skein]: 1 skein
Set of 4 double pointed knitting needles, size 2 (2.75 mm) **or** size needed for gauge
Split-ring marker
Tapestry needle

GAUGE: In Stockinette Stitch, 16 sts and 20 rnds = 2" (5 cm)

✓ *Take the time to check your gauge.*

Techniques used:
• YO *(Fig. 4, page 91)*
• K2 tog *(Fig. 9, page 92)*
• SSK *(Figs. 12a-c, page 92)*
• P2 tog *(Fig. 15, page 93)*

CUFF

Picot cast on: Place a slip knot on needle, cable cast on 4 sts *(Figs. 1a & b, page 90)*, bind off 3 sts, slip st from right hand needle to left hand needle; ★ cable cast on 5 sts, bind off 3 sts, slip st from right hand needle to left hand needle; repeat from ★ until you have 30{30, 36} sts.

Knit 1 row.

Divide stitches evenly onto 3 needles, placing 10{10, 12} sts on each needle.

Place a marker around the first stitch and join for working in the round, being careful not to twist stitches *(see Double Pointed Needles, page 90)*.

Work in K1, P1 ribbing for 6 rnds.

LEG

Rnds 1-3: Knit around.

Rnd 4: ★ K1, K2 tog, YO, K1, YO, SSK; repeat from ★ around.

Rnds 5-7: Knit around.

Rnd 8: ★ K1, K2 tog, YO, K1, YO, SSK; repeat from ★ around.

Rnds 9-12: Knit around.

Rnds 13-21: Repeat Rnds 4-12.

Lace Pattern

						9
	\	o		o	/	8
						7
						6
						5
	\	o		o	/	4
						3
						2
						1

6-st repeat

Key

□ knit

o YO

⧄ K2 tog

⧅ SSK

HEEL

Dividing Row: Knit across Needle 1, with same needle, knit 6 sts from Needle 2; slip remaining sts from Needle 2 onto Needle 3 and leave these 14{14, 18} sts unworked for Instep.

The Heel Flap will be worked back and forth in rows across the first 16{16, 18} stitches.

HEEL FLAP

Row 1 (Wrong side): Slip 1 purlwise with yarn in front, purl across; turn.

Row 2: Slip 1 knitwise with yarn in back, knit across; turn.

Repeat Rows 1 and 2, 7{7, 8} times.

HEEL TURNING

Begin working in short rows as follows:

Row 1 (Wrong side): P 10{10, 11}, P2 tog, P1, leave remaining 3{3, 4} sts unworked; **turn.**

Continuing to slip the first stitch holding yarn to **wrong** side, slip knitwise on all **right** side rows and purlwise on all **wrong** side rows.

Row 2: Slip 1, K5, SSK, K1; turn.

Row 3: Slip 1, P6, P2 tog, P1; turn.

Row 4: Slip 1, K7, SSK, K1; turn.

Sizes 3-6 months and 6-12 months Only
Row 5: Slip 1, P8, P2 tog; turn.

Row 6: Slip 1, K8, SSK: 10 sts.

Size 18-24 months Only
Row 5: Slip 1, P8, P2 tog, P1; turn.

Row 6: Slip 1, K9, SSK, K1: 12 sts.

GUSSET

Rnd 1: With **right** side of Heel facing and using needle holding Heel sts (Needle 1), pick up 8{8, 9} sts along edge of Heel Flap *(Fig. 17, page 93)*; with empty needle, pick up 1{1, 0} st(s) in gap between Heel Flap and Instep *(see Zeros, page 89)*, knit 14{14, 18} Instep sts, pick up 1{1, 0} st(s) in gap between Instep and Heel Flap (Needle 2); with empty needle, pick up 8{8, 9} sts along edge of Heel Flap, knit first 5{5, 6} sts of Heel from Needle 1 (Needle 3), place marker around next st to indicate beginning of rnd: 42{42, 48} sts, arranged 13-16-13 {13-16-13, 15-18-15}.

Rnd 2 (Decrease rnd): On Needle 1, knit across needle to last 3 sts, K2 tog, K1; on Needle 2, knit across; on Needle 3, K1, SSK, knit across: 40{40, 46} sts.

Rnd 3: Knit around.

Repeat Rnds 2 and 3, 4{4, 5} times: 32{32, 36} sts, arranged 8-16-8 {8-16-8, 9-18-9}.

FOOT

Knit each round until Foot measures approximately 2½{2¾, 3¼}"/6.5{7, 8.5} cm from back of Heel, **or** about 1{1, 1¼}"/2.5{2.5, 3} cm shorter than desired length of Sock.

TOE

Rnd 1 (Decrease rnd): On Needle 1, knit across needle to last 3 sts, K2 tog, K1; on Needle 2, K1, SSK, knit across needle to last 3 sts, K2 tog, K1; on Needle 3, K1, SSK, knit across: 28{28, 32} sts.

Rnd 2: Knit around.

Repeat Rnds 1 and 2, 4{4, 5} times: 12 sts.

FINISHING

With Needle 3, knit sts from Needle 1: 6 sts on both needles.

With tapestry needle, graft Toe *(Figs. 18a & b, page 94)*. Weave in ends.

BABY RIB SOCKS

◖■■■▢ INTERMEDIATE

Baby Sizes	Finished Foot Circumference		Finished Foot Length	
3-6 months	4"	(10 cm)	3½"	(9 cm)
6-12 months	4"	(10 cm)	3¾"	(9.5 cm)
18-24 months	4½"	(11.5 cm)	4½"	(11.5 cm)

Size Note: Instructions are written for size 3-6 months with sizes 6-12 months and 18-24 months in braces { }. Instructions will be easier to read if you circle all the numbers pertaining to your size. If only one number is given, it applies to all sizes.

MATERIALS
Super Fine Weight Yarn [SUPER FINE 1]
[3.5 ounces, 435 yards
(100 grams, 398 meters) per
hank]: 1 hank
Set of 4 double pointed knitting
  needles, size 2 (2.75 mm) **or** size
  needed for gauge
Split-ring marker
Tapestry needle

GAUGE: In Stockinette Stitch,
  16 sts and 20 rnds =
  2" (5 cm)
✔ *Take the time to check your gauge.*

Techniques used:
• tbl *(Fig. 3, page 91)*
• K2 tog *(Fig. 9, page 92)*
• SSK *(Figs. 12a-c, page 92)*
• P2 tog *(Fig. 15, page 93)*

CUFF

Cast on 32{32, 36} sts loosely.

Divide stitches evenly onto 3 needles, arranged 11-10-11{11-10-11, 12-12-12}.

Place a marker around the first stitch and join for working in the round, being careful not to twist stitches *(see Double Pointed Needles, page 90)*.

Rnds 1-3: ★ K2-tbl, P2; repeat from ★ around.

Rnds 4 and 5: Purl around.

Rnds 6-20: Repeat Rnds 1-5, 3 times for Twisted Rib pattern.

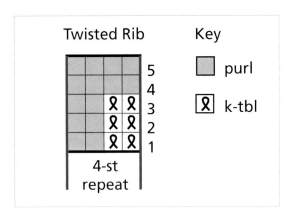

HEEL

Dividing Row: Knit across Needle 1, with same needle, knit 5{5-6} sts from Needle 2; slip remaining sts from Needle 2 onto Needle 3 and leave these 16{16, 18} sts unworked for Instep.

The Heel Flap will be worked back and forth in rows across the first 16{16, 18} stitches.

HEEL FLAP

Row 1 (Wrong side): Slip 1 purlwise with yarn in front, purl across; turn.

Row 2: Slip 1 knitwise with yarn in back, knit across; turn.

Repeat Rows 1 and 2, 7{7, 8} times.

HEEL TURNING

Begin working in short rows as follows:

Row 1 (Wrong side): P 10{10, 11}, P2 tog, P1, leave remaining 3{3, 4} sts unworked; **turn.**

Continuing to slip the first stitch holding yarn to **wrong** side, slip knitwise on all **right** side rows and purlwise on all **wrong** side rows.

Row 2: Slip 1, K5, SSK, K1; turn.

Row 3: Slip 1, P6, P2 tog, P1; turn.

Row 4: Slip 1, K7, SSK, K1; turn.

Sizes 3-6 months and 6-12 months Only
Row 5: Slip 1, P8, P2 tog; turn.

Row 6: Slip 1, K8, SSK: 10 sts.

Size 18-24 months Only
Row 5: Slip 1, P8, P2 tog, P1; turn.

Row 6: Slip 1, K9, SSK, K1: 12 sts.

GUSSET
Rnd 1: With **right** side of Heel facing and using needle holding Heel sts (Needle 1), pick up 8{8, 9} sts along edge of Heel Flap *(Fig. 17, page 93)*; with empty needle, knit 16{16, 18} Instep sts (Needle 2); with empty needle, pick up 8{8, 9} sts along edge of Heel Flap, knit first 5{5, 6} sts of Heel from Needle 1 (Needle 3), place marker around next st to indicate beginning of rnd: 42{42, 48} sts, arranged 13-16-13 {13-16-13, 15-18-15}.

Rnd 2 (Decrease rnd): On Needle 1, knit across needle to last 3 sts, K2 tog, K1; on Needle 2, knit across; on Needle 3, K1, SSK, knit across: 40{40, 46} sts.

Rnd 3: Knit around.

Repeat Rnds 2 and 3, 4{4, 5} times: 32{32, 36} sts, arranged 8-16-8 {8-16-8, 9-18-9}.

FOOT
Knit each round until Foot measures approximately 2¹⁄₂{2³⁄₄, 3¹⁄₂}"/6.5{7, 9} cm from back of Heel, **or** about 1" (2.5 cm) shorter than desired length of Sock.

TOE
Rnd 1 (Decrease rnd): On Needle 1, knit across needle to last 3 sts, K2 tog, K1; on Needle 2, K1, SSK, knit across needle to last 3 sts, K2 tog, K1; on Needle 3, K1, SSK, knit across: 28{28, 32} sts.

Rnd 2: Knit around.

Repeat Rnds 1 and 2, 4{4, 5} times: 12 sts.

FINISHING
With Needle 3, knit sts from Needle 1: 6 sts on both needles.

With tapestry needle, graft Toe *(Figs. 18a & b, page 94)*. Weave in ends.

SIMPLE SLIP STITCH SOCKS

◼◼◼◻ INTERMEDIATE

Sizes	Finished Foot Circumference		Finished Foot Length	
Child				
Small	5"	(12.5 cm)	5½"	(14 cm)
Medium	5¾"	(14.5 cm)	7½"	(19 cm)
Large	7"	(18 cm)	8"	(20.5 cm)
Adult				
Man	8"	(20.5 cm)	11"	(28 cm)

Size Note: Child sizes to fit ages 2-4, 6-8, and 10-12. The Child's size Large can easily be made to fit a woman by making the foot length longer *(see Sizing, page 89)*.

Instructions are written for Child's size Small, with Child's sizes Medium and Large and Man's size in braces { }. Instructions will be easier to read if you circle all the numbers pertaining to your size. If only one number is given, it applies to all sizes.

MATERIALS

Super Fine Weight Yarn **SUPER FINE 1**
[1.75 ounces, 166 yards
(50 grams, 152 meters) per skein]:
1{2, 2, 2} skein(s)
Set of 4 double pointed knitting
needles, size 3 (3.25 mm) **or** size
needed for gauge
Split-ring marker
Tapestry needle

GAUGE: In Stockinette Stitch and
in Slip Stitch pattern,
14 sts and 20 rnds =
2" (5 cm)

✔ *Take the time to check your gauge.*

Techniques used:
• K2 tog *(Fig. 9, page 92)*
• SSK *(Figs. 12a-c, page 92)*
• P2 tog *(Fig. 15, page 93)*

CUFF

Cast on 36{40, 48, 56} sts loosely.

Divide stitches onto 3 needles, arranged 12-12-12 {13-14-13, 16-16-16, 19-18-19}.

Place a marker around the first stitch and join for working in the round, being careful not to twist stitches *(see Double Pointed Needles, page 90)*.

Work in K1, P1 ribbing until Sock measures 1{1, 1, 1½}"/2.5{2.5, 2.5, 4} cm from cast on edge.

LEG

Rnds 1 and 2: ★ Slip 1 purlwise with yarn in back, K3; repeat from ★ around.

Rnds 3 and 4: Knit around.

Repeat Rnds 1-4 for Simple Slip Stitch pattern until Sock measures approximately 3{4, 5, 7}"/ 7.5{10, 12.5, 18} cm from cast on edge.

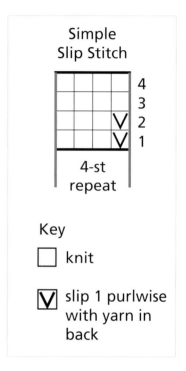

Simple
Slip Stitch

			4
			3
		V	2
		V	1

4-st repeat

Key

☐ knit

☑ slip 1 purlwise with yarn in back

HEEL

Dividing Row: Knit across Needle 1, with same needle, knit 6{7, 8, 9} sts from Needle 2; slip remaining sts from Needle 2 onto Needle 3 and leave these 18{20, 24, 28} sts unworked for Instep.

The Heel Flap will be worked back and forth in rows across the first 18{20, 24, 28} stitches.

HEEL FLAP

Row 1 (Wrong side): Slip 1 purlwise with yarn in front, purl across; turn.

Row 2: Slip 1 knitwise with yarn in back, knit across; turn.

Repeat Rows 1 and 2, 8{9, 11, 13} times.

HEEL TURNING

Begin working in short rows as follows:

Row 1 (Wrong side): P 11{12, 14, 16}, P2 tog, P1, leave remaining 4{5, 7, 9} sts unworked; **turn.**

Continuing to slip the first stitch holding yarn to **wrong** side, slip knitwise on all **right** side rows and purlwise on all **wrong** side rows.

Row 2: Slip 1, K5, SSK, K1; turn.

Row 3: Slip 1, P6, P2 tog, P1; turn.

Row 4: Slip 1, K7, SSK, K1; turn.

Row 5: Slip 1, P8, P2 tog, P1; turn.

Row 6: Slip 1, K9, SSK, K1; turn.

Child's Size Small Only
Row 7: Slip 1, P9, P2 tog; turn.

Row 8: Slip 1, K8, SSK: 10 sts.

Child's Size Medium Only
Row 7: Slip 1, P 10, P2 tog; turn.

Row 8: Slip 1, K 10, SSK: 12 sts.

Child's Size Large Only
Row 7: Slip 1, P 10, P2 tog, P1; turn.

Row 8: Slip 1, K 11, SSK, K1; turn.

Row 9: Slip 1, P 12, P2 tog; turn.

Row 10: Slip 1, K 12, SSK: 14 sts.

Man's Size Only
Row 7: Slip 1, P 10, P2 tog, P1; turn.

Row 8: Slip 1, K 11, SSK, K1; turn.

Row 9: Slip 1, P 12, P2 tog, P1; turn.

Row 10: Slip 1, K 13, SSK, K1; turn.

Row 11: Slip 1, P 14, P2 tog; turn.

Row 12: Slip 1, K 14, SSK: 16 sts.

GUSSET

Rnd 1: With **right** side of Heel facing and using needle holding Heel sts (Needle 1), pick up 9{10, 12, 14} sts along edge of Heel Flap *(Fig. 17, page 93)*, pick up one st in gap between Heel Flap and Instep; with empty needle, knit 18{20, 24, 28} Instep sts (Needle 2); with empty needle, pick up one st in gap between Instep and Heel Flap, pick up 9{10, 12, 14} sts along edge of Heel Flap, knit first 5{6, 7, 8} sts of Heel from Needle 1 (Needle 3), place marker around next st to indicate beginning of rnd: 48{54, 64, 74} sts, arranged 15-18-15 {17-20-17, 20-24-20, 23-28-23}.

Continued on page 63.

EYELET SQUARES SOCKS

Child Sizes	Finished Foot Circumference		Finished Foot Length	
Small	5"	(12.5 cm)	5½"	(14 cm)
Medium	6"	(15 cm)	7½"	(19 cm)
Large	7"	(18 cm)	8"	(20.5 cm)

Size Note: To fit children ages 2-4, 6-8, and 10-12. The size large can easily be made to fit a woman by making the foot length longer *(see Sizing, page 89)*.

Instructions are written for size Small with sizes Medium and Large in braces { }. Instructions will be easier to read if you circle all the numbers pertaining to your size. If only one number is given, it applies to all sizes.

MATERIALS

Super Fine Weight Yarn **SUPER FINE 1**
[3. 5 ounces, 435 yards (100 grams, 398 meters) per hank]: 1 hank
Set of 4 double pointed knitting needles, size 2 (2.75 mm) **or** size needed for gauge
Split-ring marker
Tapestry needle

GAUGE: In Stockinette Stitch, 16 sts and 22 rnds = 2" (5 cm)

✔ *Take the time to check your gauge.*

Techniques used:
• YO *(Fig. 4, page 91)*
• M1 *(Figs. 5a & b, page 91)*
• K2 tog *(Fig. 9, page 92)*
• SSK *(Figs. 12a-c, page 92)*
• Slip 1 as if to **knit**, K2 tog, PSSO *(Fig. 14, page 93)*
• P2 tog *(Fig. 15, page 93)*

EYELET SQUARES (multiple of 6 sts)
Rnds 1 and 2: Knit around.
Rnd 3: ★ K3, YO, slip 1 as if to knit, K2 tog, PSSO, YO; repeat from ★ around.
Rnd 4: ★ K3, P1, K1, P1; repeat from ★ around.
Rnds 5 and 6: Knit around.
Rnd 7: ★ YO, slip 1 as if to knit, K2 tog, PSSO, YO, K3; repeat from ★ around.
Rnd 8: ★ P1, K1, P1, K3; repeat from ★ around.
Repeat Rnds 1-8 for Eyelet Squares pattern.

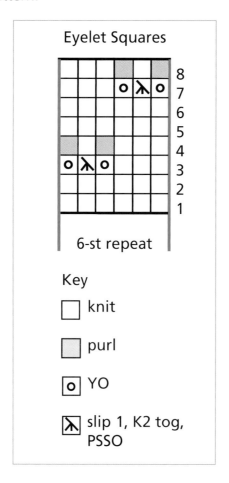

Eyelet Squares

6-st repeat

Key

□ knit

▨ purl

◙ YO

⋏ slip 1, K2 tog, PSSO

CUFF

Cast on 42{48, 54} sts loosely.

Divide stitches evenly onto 3 needles, placing 14{16, 18} on each.

Place a marker around the first stitch and join for working in the round, being careful not to twist stitches *(see Double Pointed Needles, page 90)*.

Work in K1, P1 ribbing until Sock measures 1{1, 1$^1/_4$}"/2.5{2.5, 3} cm from cast on edge.

LEG

Work in Eyelet Squares pattern until Sock measures approximately 3{4, 5}"/7.5{10, 12.5} cm from cast on edge, ending by working Rnd 4 or Rnd 8 of pattern.

HEEL

Dividing Row: Knit across Needle 1, with same needle, knit 7{5, 9} sts from Needle 2; slip remaining sts from Needle 2 onto Needle 3 and leave these 21{27, 27} sts unworked for Instep.

The Heel Flap will be worked back and forth in rows across the first 21{21, 27} stitches.

HEEL FLAP

Sizes Small and Large Only

Row 1 (Wrong side): Slip 1 purlwise with yarn in front, P 9{12}, P2 tog, P 9{12}; turn: 20{26} sts.

Size Medium Only

Row 1 (Wrong side): Slip 1 purlwise with yarn in front, P9, purl in front and back of next st, P 10; turn: 22 sts.

All Sizes

Row 2: Slip 1 purlwise with yarn in back, knit across; turn.

Row 3: Slip 1 purlwise with yarn in front, purl across; turn.

Repeat Rows 2 and 3, 8{9, 11} times; then repeat Row 2 once **more**.

HEEL TURNING

Begin working in short rows as follows:

Row 1 (Wrong side): P 12{13, 15}, P2 tog, P1, leave remaining 5{6, 8} sts unworked; **turn**.

Continuing to slip the first stitch holding yarn to **wrong** side, slip knitwise on all **right** side rows and purlwise on all **wrong** side rows.

Row 2: Slip 1, K5, SSK, K1; turn.

Row 3: Slip 1, P6, P2 tog, P1; turn.

Row 4: Slip 1, K7, SSK, K1; turn.

Row 5: Slip 1, P8, P2 tog, P1; turn.

Row 6: Slip 1, K9, SSK, K1; turn.

Size Small Only

Row 7: Slip 1, P 10, P2 tog; turn.

Row 8: Slip 1, K 10, SSK: 12 sts.

Size Medium Only

Row 7: Slip 1, P 10, P2 tog, P1; turn.

Row 8: Slip 1, K 11, SSK, K1: 14 sts.

Size Large Only

Row 7: Slip 1, P 10, P2 tog, P1; turn.

Row 8: Slip 1, K 11, SSK, K1; turn.

Row 9: Slip 1, P 12, P2 tog, P1; turn.

Row 10: Slip 1, K 13, SSK, K1: 16 sts.

GUSSET

Rnd 1: With **right** side of Heel facing and using needle holding Heel sts (Needle 1), pick up 10{11, 13} sts along edge of Heel Flap *(Fig. 17, page 93)*, pick up one st in gap between Heel Flap and Instep; with empty needle, knit 21{27, 27} Instep sts (Needle 2); with empty needle, pick up one st in gap between Instep and Heel Flap, pick up 10{11, 13} sts along edge of Heel Flap, knit first 6{7, 8} sts of Heel from Needle 1 (Needle 3), place marker around next st to indicate beginning of rnd: 55{65, 71} sts, arranged 17-21-17 {19-27-19, 22-27-22}.

Rnd 2 (Decrease rnd): On Needle 1, knit across needle to last 2 sts, K2 tog; on Needle 2, K3, work across in Eyelet Squares pattern to last 3 sts, K3; on Needle 3, SSK, knit across: 53{63, 69} sts.

Rnd 3: On Needle 1, knit across; on Needle 2, K3, work across in Eyelet Squares pattern to last 3 sts, K3; on Needle 3, knit across.

Continued on page 63.

BUTTERFLY BOWS SOCKS

●■■■▢ INTERMEDIATE

Child Sizes	Finished Foot Circumference		Finished Foot Length	
Medium	5³/₄"	(14.5 cm)	7¹/₂"	(19 cm)
Large	7"	(18 cm)	8"	(20.5 cm)

Size Note: To fit children ages 6-8 and 10-12. The size Large can easily be made to fit a woman by making the foot length longer *(see Sizing, page 89)*.

Instructions are written for size Medium with size Large in braces { }. Instructions will be easier to read if you circle all the numbers pertaining to your size. If only one number is given, it applies to both sizes.

MATERIALS
Light Weight Yarn **③**
[3.5 ounces, 306 yards
(100 grams, 280 meters) per skein]:
  1 skein
Set of 4 double pointed knitting
  needles, size 3 (3.25 mm) **or** size
  needed for gauge
Split-ring marker
Tapestry needle

GAUGE: In Stockinette Stitch,
  14 sts and 19 rnds =
  2" (5 cm)
✓ *Take the time to check your gauge.*

Techniques used:
• K2 tog *(Fig. 9, page 92)*
• SSK *(Figs. 12a-c, page 92)*
• P2 tog *(Fig. 15, page 93)*

BUTTERFLY BOWS (multiple of 10 sts)
Rnd 1: Knit around.
Rnd 2: ★ K5, slip 5 sts purlwise with yarn in front; repeat from ★ around.
Rnds 3-6: Repeat Rnds 1 and 2 twice.
Rnd 7: K7, insert right hand needle tip under 3 floats from previous rnds, K1 from left needle catching floats, ★ K9, insert right hand needle tip under 3 floats from previous rnds, K1 from left needle catching floats; repeat from ★ around to last 2 sts, K2.
Rnd 8: Knit around.
Rnd 9: Knit around.
Rnd 10: ★ Slip 5 sts purlwise with yarn in front, K5; repeat from ★ around.
Rnds 11-14: Repeat Rnds 9 and 10 twice.
Rnd 15: K2, insert right hand needle tip under 3 floats from previous rnds, K1 from left needle catching floats, ★ K9, insert right hand needle tip under 3 floats from previous rnds, K1 from left needle catching floats; repeat from ★ around to last 7 sts, K7.
Rnd 16: Knit around.
Repeat Rnds 1-16 for Butterfly Bows pattern.

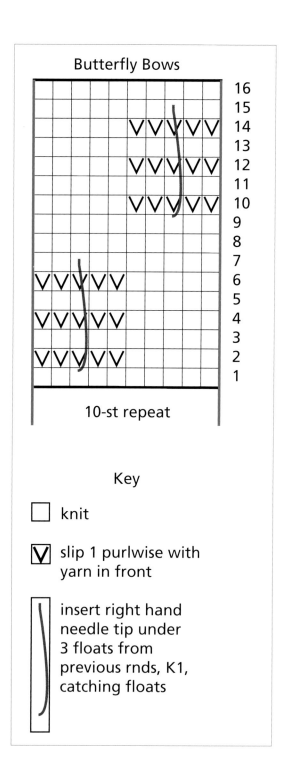

Butterfly Bows

10-st repeat

Key

☐ knit

▽ slip 1 purlwise with yarn in front

insert right hand needle tip under 3 floats from previous rnds, K1, catching floats

CUFF

Cast on 40{50} sts loosely.

Divide stitches onto 3 needles, arranged 15-10-15 {15-20-15}.

Place a marker around the first stitch and join for working in the round, being careful not to twist stitches *(see Double Pointed Needles, page 90)*.

Work in K1, P1 ribbing until Sock measures 1" (2.5 cm) from cast on edge.

LEG

Work Rnds 1-16 of Butterfly Bows stitch once, then repeat Rnds 1-8 once **more**.

HEEL

Dividing Row: Knit across Needle 1, with same needle, knit 5{10} sts from Needle 2; slip remaining sts from Needle 2 onto Needle 3 and leave these 20{25} sts unworked for Instep.

The Heel Flap will be worked back and forth in rows across the first 20{25} stitches.

HEEL FLAP

Row 1 (Wrong side): Slip 1 purlwise with yarn in front, purl across; turn.

Row 2: Slip 1 purlwise with yarn in back, knit across; turn.

Repeat Rows 1 and 2, 9{11} times, decreasing 0{1} st(s) on last row *(see Zeros, page 89)*: 20{24} sts.

HEEL TURNING

Begin working in short rows as follows:

Row 1 (Wrong side): P 12{14}, P2 tog, P1, leave remaining 5{7} sts unworked; **turn**.

Continuing to slip the first stitch holding yarn to **wrong** side, slip knitwise on all **right** side rows and purlwise on all **wrong** side rows.

Row 2: Slip 1, K5, SSK, K1; turn.

Row 3: Slip 1, P6, P2 tog, P1; turn.

Row 4: Slip 1, K7, SSK, K1; turn.

Row 5: Slip 1, P8, P2 tog, P1; turn.

Row 6: Slip 1, K9, SSK, K1; turn.

Size Medium Only
Row 7: Slip 1, P 10, P2 tog; turn.

Row 8: Slip 1, K 10, SSK: 12 sts.

Size Large Only
Row 7: Slip 1, P 10, P2 tog, P1; turn.

Row 8: Slip 1, K 11, SSK, K1; turn.

Row 9: Slip 1, P 12, P2 tog; turn.

Row 10: Slip 1, K 12, SSK: 14 sts.

BUTTERFLY BOWS SOCKS continued from page 61.

GUSSET

Rnd 1: With **right** side of Heel facing and using needle holding Heel sts (Needle 1), pick up 10{12} sts along edge of Heel Flap *(Fig. 17, page 93)*, pick up 0{1} st(s) in gap between Heel Flap and Instep; with empty needle, knit 20{25} Instep sts (Needle 2); with empty needle, pick up 10{12} sts along edge of Heel Flap, knit first 6{7} sts of Heel from Needle 1 (Needle 3), place marker around next st to indicate beginning of rnd: 52{64} sts, arranged 16-20-16 {20-25-19}.

Rnd 2 (Decrease rnd): On Needle 1, knit across needle to last 3 sts, K2 tog, K1; on Needle 2, work across in established Butterfly Bows pattern; on Needle 3, K1, SSK, knit across: 50{62} sts.

Rnd 3: On Needle 1, knit across; on Needle 2, work across in established Butterfly Bows pattern; on Needle 3, knit across.

Repeat Rnds 2 and 3, 5{6} times: 40{50} sts, arranged 10-20-10 {13-25-12}.

FOOT

Work even (Rnd 3 of Gusset) until 72 rnds of Butterfly Bows pattern have been worked from Cuff.

Knit each round until Foot measures approximately 6¼{6½}"/ 16{16.5} cm from back of Heel, **or** about 1¼{1½}"/3{4} cm shorter than desired length of Sock.

TOE

Rnd 1 (Decrease rnd): On Needle 1, knit across needle to last 3 sts, K2 tog, K1; on Needle 2, K1, SSK, knit across needle to last 3 sts, K2 tog, K1; on Needle 3, K1, SSK, knit across: 36{46} sts.

Rnd 2: Knit around.

Repeat Rnds 1 and 2, 4{5} times: 20{26} sts.

Repeat Rnd 1 only, 2{3} times: 12{14} sts.

FINISHING

With Needle 3, knit sts from Needle 1: 6{7} sts on both needles.

With tapestry needle, graft Toe *(Figs. 18a & b, page 94)*. Weave in ends.

**SIMPLE SLIP STITCH SOCKS
continued from page 53.**

Rnd 2 (Decrease rnd): On Needle 1, knit across needle to last 3 sts, K2 tog, K1; on Needle 2, knit across; on Needle 3, K1, SSK, knit across: 46{52, 62, 72} sts.

Rnd 3: Knit around.

Repeat Rnds 2 and 3, 5{6, 7, 8} times: 36{40, 48, 56} sts, arranged 9-18-9 {10-20-10, 12-24-12, 14-28-14}.

FOOT
Knit each round until Foot measures approximately 4$\frac{1}{2}${6$\frac{1}{4}$, 6$\frac{1}{2}$, 9}"/11.5{16, 16.5, 23} cm from back of Heel, **or** about 1{1$\frac{1}{4}$, 1$\frac{1}{2}$, 2}"/ 2.5{3, 4, 5} cm shorter than desired length of Sock.

TOE
Rnd 1 (Decrease rnd): On Needle 1, knit across needle to last 3 sts, K2 tog, K1; on Needle 2, K1, SSK, knit across needle to last 3 sts, K2 tog, K1; on Needle 3, K1, SSK, knit across: 32{36, 44, 52} sts.

Rnd 2: Knit around.

Repeat Rnds 1 and 2, 3{4, 5, 7} times: 20{20, 24, 24} sts.

Repeat Rnd 1 only, 2{2, 3, 3} times: 12 sts.

FINISHING
With Needle 3, knit sts from Needle 1: 6 sts on both needles.

With tapestry needle, graft Toe *(Figs. 18a & b, page 94)*. Weave in ends.

**EYELET SQUARES SOCKS
continued from page 57.**

Repeat Rnds 2 and 3, 6{7, 8} times: 41{49, 53} sts, arranged 10-21-10 {11-27-11, 13-27-13}.

FOOT
Work even (Rnd 3 of Gusset) until Foot measures approximately 4$\frac{1}{4}${6$\frac{1}{4}$, 6$\frac{3}{4}$}"/ 11{16, 17} cm from back of Heel, **or** about 1$\frac{1}{4}$" (3 cm) shorter than desired length of Sock.

**Sizes Small and Large Only
- Next Rnd:** M1, knit around: 42{54} sts.

Size Medium Only - Next Rnd: K2 tog, knit around: 48 sts.

TOE
Rnd 1: ★ K4, K2 tog; repeat from ★ around: 35{40, 45} sts.

Rnds 2-4: Knit around.

Rnd 5: ★ K3, K2 tog; repeat from ★ around: 28{32, 36} sts.

Rnds 6-8: Knit around.

Rnd 9: ★ K2, K2 tog; repeat from ★ around: 21{24, 27} sts.

Rnds 10 and 11: Knit around.

Rnd 12: ★ K1, K2 tog; repeat from ★ around: 14{16, 18} sts.

Rnd 13: Knit around.

Rnd 14: K2 tog around: 7{8, 9} sts.

Cut yarn leaving a long end for sewing. Thread tapestry needle with end and slip remaining sts onto yarn; gather tightly to close and secure end. Weave in ends.

SPIRAL RIB SOCKS

Sizes	Finished Foot Circumference		Finished Foot Length	
Child				
Small	5¼"	(13.5 cm)	5½"	(14 cm)
Medium	6"	(15 cm)	7½"	(19 cm)
Large	6¾"	(17 cm)	8"	(20.5 cm)
Adult				
Woman	7½"	(19 cm)	9½"	(24 cm)
Man	8¼"	(21 cm)	11"	(28 cm)

Size Note: Child sizes to fit ages 2-4, 6-8, and 10-12. Instructions are written with Child's sizes in the first set of braces { } and Adult sizes in the second set of braces. Instructions will be easier to read if you circle all the numbers pertaining to your size. If only one number is given, it applies to all sizes.

MATERIALS

Super Fine Weight Yarn **SUPER FINE ①**

Version 1
[1.76 ounces, 213 yards
(50 grams, 195 meters) per skein]:
  {1-1-2}{2-2} skein(s)

Version 2
[1.76 ounces, 230 yards
(50 grams, 210 meters) per skein]:
  {1-1-2}{2-2} skein(s)
Set of 4 double pointed knitting
  needles, size 2 (2.75 mm) **or** size
  needed for gauge
Split-ring marker
Tapestry needle

GAUGE: In Stockinette Stitch,
16 sts and 20 rnds =
2" (5 cm)
✓ *Take the time to check your gauge.*

Techniques used:
• M1 *(Figs. 5a & b, page 91)*
• K2 tog *(Fig. 9, page 92)*
• SSK *(Figs. 12a-c, page 92)*
• P2 tog *(Fig. 15, page 93)*

SPIRAL RIB (multiple of 6 sts)
Rnds 1-4: ★ P2, K4; repeat from ★ around.
Rnds 5-8: K2, P2, ★ K4, P2; repeat from ★ around to last 2 sts, K2.
Rnds 9-12: ★ K4, P2; repeat from ★ around.
Repeat Rnds 1-12 for Spiral Rib pattern.

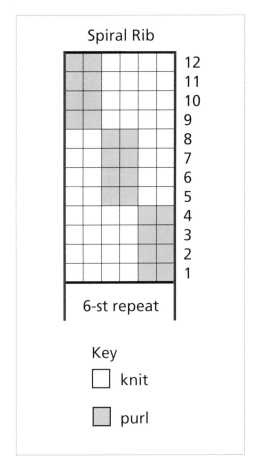

Spiral Rib

12
11
10
9
8
7
6
5
4
3
2
1

6-st repeat

Key

☐ knit

▨ purl

LEG
Cast on {42, 48, 54}{60, 66} sts loosely.

Divide stitches onto 3 needles, placing {14, 16, 18}{20, 22} on each.

Place a marker around the first stitch and join for working in the round, being careful not to twist stitches *(see Double Pointed Needles, page 90)*.

Work in Spiral Rib pattern until Leg measures approximately {3, 4, 5}{6, 7}"/{7.5, 10, 12.5}{15, 18} cm from cast on edge.

HEEL
Dividing Row: Knit across Needle 1, with same needle, knit {7, 8, 9} {10, 11} sts from Needle 2; slip remaining sts from Needle 2 onto Needle 3 and leave these {21, 24, 27} {30, 33} sts unworked for Instep.

The Heel Flap will be worked back and forth in rows across the first {21, 24, 27}{30, 33} stitches.

HEEL FLAP
Row 1 (Wrong side): Slip 1 purlwise with yarn in front, purl across; turn.

Row 2: Slip 1 purlwise with yarn in back, knit across; turn.

Repeat Rows 1 and 2,
{9, 11, 12}{14, 15} times
working M1 {1, 0, 1}{0, 1}
time(s) on last row (see Zeros,
page 89):
{22, 24, 28}{30, 34} sts.

HEEL TURNING
Begin working in short rows as
follows:

Row 1 (Wrong side):
P {13, 14, 16}{17, 19}, P2 tog,
P1, leave remaining {6, 7, 9}
{10, 12} sts unworked; turn.

Continuing to slip the first
stitch holding yarn to wrong
side, slip knitwise on all right
side rows and purlwise on all
wrong side rows.

Row 2: Slip 1, K5, SSK, K1;
turn.

Row 3: Slip 1, P6, P2 tog, P1;
turn.

Row 4: Slip 1, K7, SSK, K1;
turn.

Row 5: Slip 1, P8, P2 tog, P1;
turn.

Row 6: Slip 1, K9, SSK, K1;
turn.

Row 7: Slip 1, P 10, P2 tog, P1;
turn.

Child's Size Small Only
Row 8: Slip 1, K 11, SSK, K1:
14 sts.

Child's Size Medium Only
Row 8: Slip 1, K 11, SSK, K1;
turn.

Row 9: Slip 1, P 12, P2 tog;
turn.

Row 10: Slip 1, K 12, SSK:
14 sts.

Child's Size Large Only
Row 8: Slip 1, K 11, SSK, K1;
turn.

Row 9: Slip 1, P 12, P2 tog, P1;
turn.

Row 10: Slip 1, K 13, SSK, K1;
turn.

Row 11: Slip 1, P 14, P2 tog;
turn.

Row 12: Slip 1, K 14, SSK:
16 sts.

Woman's Size Only
Row 8: Slip 1, K 11, SSK, K1;
turn.

Row 9: Slip 1, P 12, P2 tog,
P1; turn.

Row 10: Slip 1, K 13, SSK, K1;
turn.

Row 11: Slip 1, P 14, P2 tog,
P1; turn.

Row 12: Slip 1, K 15, SSK, K1:
18 sts.

Man's Size Only
Row 8: Slip 1, K 11, SSK, K1;
turn.

Row 9: Slip 1, P 12, P2 tog,
P1; turn.

Row 10: Slip 1, K 13, SSK, K1;
turn.

Row 11: Slip 1, P 14, P2 tog,
P1; turn.

Row 12: Slip 1, K 15, SSK, K1;
turn.

Row 13: Slip 1, P 16, P2 tog,
P1; turn.

Row 14: Slip 1, K 17, SSK, K1:
20 sts.

Continued on page 73.

LEAF SOCKS

Size: Woman
Finished Foot Circumference: 7" (18 cm)
Finished Foot Length: 9" (23 cm)

Size Note: These socks can easily be made to fit children ages 10-12 by making the foot length shorter *(see Sizing, page 89)*.

MATERIALS

Light Weight Yarn 🟡**3**
[3.5 ounces, 262 yards
(100 grams, 239 meters) per hank]:
  2 hanks
Set of 4 double pointed knitting
  needles, size 3 (3.25 mm) **or** size
  needed for gauge
Split-ring marker
Tapestry needle

GAUGE: In Stockinette Stitch,
     14 sts and 19 rnds =
     2" (5 cm)
✔ *Take the time to check your gauge.*

Techniques used:
- YO *(Fig. 4, page 91)*
- K2 tog *(Fig. 9, page 92)*
- SSK *(Figs. 12a-c, page 92)*
- Slip 1 as if to **knit**, K2 tog, PSSO *(Fig. 14, page 93)*
- P2 tog *(Fig. 15, page 93)*

CUFF

Cast on 48 sts loosely.

Divide stitches evenly onto 3 needles, placing 16 on each.

Place a marker around the first stitch and join for working in the round, being careful not to twist stitches *(see Double Pointed Needles, page 90)*.

Work in K2, P2 ribbing until Sock measures 1" (2.5 cm) from cast on edge.

LEG

Knit each round until Sock measures approximately 5" (12.5 cm) from cast on edge.

HEEL

Dividing Row: Knit across Needle 1, with same needle, knit 8 sts from Needle 2; slip remaining sts from Needle 2 onto Needle 3 and leave these 24 sts unworked for Instep.

The Heel Flap will be worked back and forth in rows across the first 24 stitches.

HEEL FLAP

Row 1 (Wrong side): Slip 1 purlwise with yarn in front, purl across; turn.

Row 2: ★ Slip 1 purlwise with yarn in back, K1; repeat from ★ across; turn.

Repeat Rows 1 and 2, 11 times.

HEEL TURNING

Begin working in short rows as follows:

Row 1 (Wrong side): P 14, P2 tog, P1, leave remaining 7 sts unworked; **turn**.

Continuing to slip the first stitch holding yarn to **wrong** side, slip knitwise on all **right** side rows and purlwise on all **wrong** side rows.

Row 2: Slip 1, K5, SSK, K1; turn.

Row 3: Slip 1, P6, P2 tog, P1; turn.

Row 4: Slip 1, K7, SSK, K1; turn.

Row 5: Slip 1, P8, P2 tog, P1; turn.

Row 6: Slip 1, K9, SSK, K1; turn.

Row 7: Slip 1, P 10, P2 tog, P1; turn.

Row 8: Slip 1, K 11, SSK, K1; turn.

Row 9: Slip 1, P 12, P2 tog; turn.

Row 10: Slip 1, K 12, SSK: 14 sts.

GUSSET

Rnd 1: With **right** side of Heel facing and using needle holding Heel sts (Needle 1), pick up 12 sts along edge of Heel Flap *(Fig. 17, page 93)*; with empty needle, knit 24 Instep sts (Needle 2); with empty needle, pick up 12 sts along edge of Heel Flap, knit first 7 sts of Heel from Needle 1 (Needle 3), place marker around next st to indicate beginning of rnd: 62 sts, arranged 19-24-19.

Rnd 2 (Decrease rnd): On Needle 1, knit across needle to last 3 sts, K2 tog, K1; on Needle 2, knit across; on Needle 3, K1, SSK, knit across: 60 sts.

Rnd 3: Knit around.

Repeat Rnds 2 and 3, 6 times: 48 sts, arranged 12-24-12.

FOOT

Knit each round until Foot measures approximately 7¹⁄₂" (19 cm) from back of Heel, **or** about 1¹⁄₂" (4 cm) shorter than desired length of Sock.

TOE

Rnd 1 (Decrease rnd): On Needle 1, knit across needle to last 3 sts, K2 tog, K1; on Needle 2, K1, SSK, knit across needle to last 3 sts, K2 tog, K1; on Needle 3, K1, SSK, knit across: 44 sts.

Rnd 2: Knit around.

Repeat Rnds 1 and 2, 5 times: 24 sts.

Repeat Rnd 1 only, 3 times: 12 sts.

FINISHING

With Needle 3, knit sts from Ncedle 1. 6 sts on both needles.

With tapestry needle, graft Toe *(Figs. 18a & b, page 94)*. Weave in ends.

LEAF (Make 4 for each Sock) Leaving a 12" (30.5 cm) end for sewing, cast on 7 sts. (See Chart, page 72 for reference.)

Row 1 (Right side): K3, YO, K1, YO, K3: 9 sts.

Row 2: Purl across.

Row 3: K3, (YO, K3) twice: 11 sts.

Row 4: Purl across.

Row 5: K3, YO, K5, YO, K3: 13 sts.

Row 6: Purl across.

Row 7: Bind off 3 sts, K2, YO, K1, YO, K6: 12 sts.

Row 8: Bind off 3 sts, purl across: 9 sts.

Rows 9-12: Repeat Rows 3-6.

Row 13: Bind off 4 sts, (K1, YO) twice, K6: 11 sts.

Row 14: Bind off 4 sts, purl across: 7 sts.

Row 15: SSK, YO, slip 2 tog as if to knit, K1, pass 2 slipped sts over knit st, YO, K2 tog: 5 sts.

Row 16: P5.

Row 17: SSK, K1, K2 tog: 3 sts.

Row 18: P3.

Row 19: Slip 1, K2 tog, PSSO; finish off.

LEAF SOCKS continued from page 71.

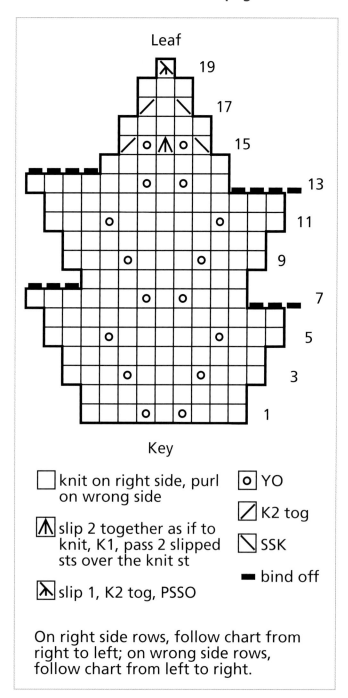

Leaf

19

17

15

13

11

9

7

5

3

1

Key

⬜ knit on right side, purl on wrong side

🔘 YO

◢ K2 tog

◣ SSK

⬛ bind off

Ⓜ slip 2 together as if to knit, K1, pass 2 slipped sts over the knit st

ⵥ slip 1, K2 tog, PSSO

On right side rows, follow chart from right to left; on wrong side rows, follow chart from left to right.

To attach Leaves, thread the tapestry needle with the long end at cast on edge. Place the **wrong** side of the Leaf on the **right** side of the Sock with cast on edge of the Leaf just below the Cuff. Sew cast on edge of Leaf to Stockinette Stitch as follows:

★ Bring the needle over the top of the stitch on the sock *(Fig. D)* then back over the cast on sts of the Leaf and pick up the inverted V of the next stitch *(Fig. E)*; repeat from ★ across Leaf *(Fig. F)*.

Fig. D

Fig. E

Fig. F

Attach 3 more leaves to the same Sock, skipping 5 sts between Leaves.

Repeat for second Sock. Weave in ends.

SPIRAL RIB SOCKS continued from page 67.

GUSSET
Rnd 1: With **right** side of Heel facing and using needle holding Heel sts (Needle 1), pick up {10, 12, 13}{15, 16} sts along edge of Heel Flap *(Fig. 17, page 93)*; with empty needle, pick up {1, 0, 1}{0, 1} st(s) in gap between Heel Flap and Instep, work {21, 24, 27}{30, 33} Instep sts in established Spiral Rib pattern (Needle 2); with empty needle, pick up {10, 12, 13}{15, 16} sts along edge of Heel Flap, knit first {7, 7, 8}{9, 10} sts of Heel from Needle 1 (Needle 3), place marker around next st to indicate beginning of rnd: {56, 62, 70}{78, 86} sts, arranged {17-22-17, 19-24-19, 21-28-21}{24-30-24, 26-34-26}.

Rnd 2 (Decrease rnd): On Needle 1, knit across needle to last 3 sts, K2 tog, K1; on Needle 2, work across in established Spiral Rib pattern; on Needle 3, K1, SSK, knit across: {54, 60, 68}{76, 84} sts.

Rnd 3: On Needle 1, knit across; on Needle 2, work across in established Spiral Rib pattern; on Needle 3, knit across.

Repeat Rnds 2 and 3, {6, 6, 7}{8, 9} times: {42, 48, 54}{60, 66} sts, arranged {10-22-10, 12-24-12, 13-28-13}{15-30-15, 16-34-16}.

FOOT
Work even (Rnd 3 of Gusset) until Foot measures approximately {4¼, 6, 6½}{7½, 9}"/{11, 15, 16.5}{19, 23} cm from back of Heel, **or** about {1¼, 1½, 1½}{2, 2}"/ {3, 4, 4}{5, 5} cm shorter than desired length of Sock.

TOE
Child's Sizes Small and Large and Man's Size Only: Slip one stitch from Needle 2 to Needle 1.

All Sizes
Rnd 1 (Decrease rnd): On Needle 1, knit across needle to last 3 sts, K2 tog, K1; on Needle 2, K1, SSK, knit across needle to last 3 sts, K2 tog, K1; on Needle 3, K1, SSK, knit across: {38, 44, 50}{56, 62} sts.

Rnd 2: Knit around.

Repeat Rnds 1 and 2, {4, 4, 5}{6, 7} times: {22, 28, 30}{32, 34} sts.

Repeat Rnd 1 only, {3, 4, 4}{4, 4} times: {10, 12, 14}{16, 18} sts.

FINISHING
With Needle 3, knit sts from Needle 1: {5, 6, 7}{8, 9} sts on both needles.

With tapestry needle, graft Toe *(Figs. 18a & b, page 94)*. Weave in ends.

CABLE RIB SOCKS

◼◼◼◻ INTERMEDIATE

Size: Woman
Finished Foot Circumference: 7" (18 cm)
Finished Foot Length: 9½" (24 cm)

Size Note: These socks can easily be made to fit children ages 10-12 by making the foot length shorter *(see Sizing, page 89)*.

MATERIALS

SUPER FINE 1

Super Fine Weight Yarn [1.75 ounces, 191 yards (50 grams, 175 meters) per hank]: 2 hanks
Set of 4 double pointed knitting needles, size 2 (2.75 mm) **or** size needed for gauge
Split-ring marker
Cable needle
Tapestry needle

GAUGE: In Stockinette Stitch, 16 sts and 22 rnds = 2" (5 cm)

✓ *Take the time to check your gauge.*

Techniques used:
• K2 tog *(Fig. 9, page 92)*
• SSK *(Figs. 12a-c, page 92)*
• P2 tog *(Fig. 15, page 93)*

LEFT SOCK
LEG
Cast on 60 sts loosely.

Divide stitches evenly onto 3 needles, placing 20 on each.

Place a marker around the first stitch and join for working in the round, being careful not to twist stitches *(see Double Pointed Needles, page 90)*.

(see Double Pointed Needles, page 90)

To work 3/3 RC *(3 over 3 Right Cross;* uses 6 sts*)*, slip next 3 sts onto cable needle and hold in **back** of work, K3 from left needle, K3 from cable needle.

Rnds 1 and 2: ★ K6, P2, K2, P2; repeat from ★ around.

Rnd 3: ★ 3/3 RC, P2, K2, P2; repeat from ★ around.

Rnds 4-10: ★ K6, P2, K2, P2; repeat from ★ around.

Repeat Rnds 3-10 for Right Cable Rib pattern until Sock measures approximately 6" (15 cm) from cast on edge.

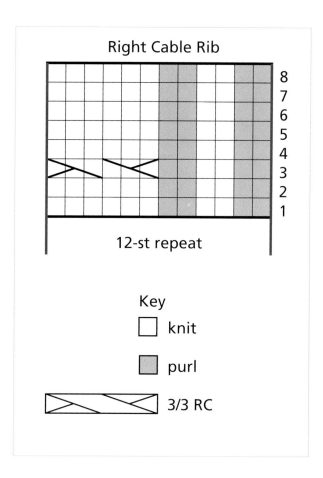

Right Cable Rib

8
7
6
5
4
3
2
1

12-st repeat

Key

☐ knit

▨ purl

▧ 3/3 RC

HEEL
Dividing Row: Knit across Needle 1, with same needle, knit 10 sts from Needle 2; slip remaining sts from Needle 2 onto Needle 3 and leave these 30 sts unworked for Instep.

The Heel Flap will be worked back and forth in rows across the first 30 stitches.

HEEL FLAP

Row 1 (Wrong side): Slip 1 purlwise with yarn in front, purl across; turn.

Row 2: ★ Slip 1 purlwise with yarn in back, knit across; turn.

Repeat Rows 1 and 2, 14 times.

HEEL TURNING

Begin working in short rows as follows:

Row 1 (Wrong side): P 17, P2 tog, P1, leave remaining 10 sts unworked; **turn**.

Continuing to slip the first stitch holding yarn to **wrong** side, slip knitwise on all **right** side rows and purlwise on all **wrong** side rows.

Row 2: Slip 1, K5, SSK, K1; turn.

Row 3: Slip 1, P6, P2 tog, P1; turn.

Row 4: Slip 1, K7, SSK, K1; turn.

Row 5: Slip 1, P8, P2 tog, P1; turn.

Row 6: Slip 1, K9, SSK, K1; turn.

Row 7: Slip 1, P 10, P2 tog, P1; turn.

Row 8: Slip 1, K 11, SSK, K1; turn.

Row 9: Slip 1, P 12, P2 tog, P1; turn.

Row 10: Slip 1, K 13, SSK, K1; turn.

Row 11: Slip 1, P 14, P2 tog, P1; turn.

Row 12: Slip 1, K 15, SSK, K1: 18 sts.

GUSSET

Rnd 1: With **right** side of Heel facing and using needle holding Heel sts (Needle 1), pick up 15 sts along edge of Heel Flap *(Fig. 17, page 93)*, pick up one st in gap between Heel Flap and Instep; with empty needle, work 30 Instep sts in established Cable Rib pattern (Needle 2); with empty needle, pick up one st in gap between Instep and Heel Flap, pick up 15 sts along edge of Heel Flap, knit first 9 sts of Heel from Needle 1 (Needle 3), place marker around next st to indicate beginning of rnd: 80 sts, arranged 25-30-25.

Rnd 2 (Decrease rnd): On Needle 1, knit across needle to last 3 sts, K2 tog, K1; on Needle 2, work across in established Cable Rib pattern; on Needle 3, K1, SSK, knit across: 78 sts.

Rnd 3: On Needle 1, knit across; on Needle 2, work across in established Cable Rib pattern; on Needle 3, knit across.

Repeat Rnds 2 and 3, 9 times: 60 sts, arranged 15-30-15.

FOOT

Work even (Rnd 3 of Gusset) until Foot measures approximately 7³/₄" (19.5 cm) from back of Heel, **or** about 1³/₄" (4.5 cm) shorter than desired length of Sock.

Continued on page 83.

GARTER SLIP STITCH SOCKS

◼◼◼◻ INTERMEDIATE

The Garter Slip Stitch pattern can be worked in three different color options, for three different looks.

Size: Woman
Finished Foot Circumference: 7" (18 cm)
Finished Foot Length: 9" (23 cm)

Size Note: These socks can easily be made to fit children ages 10-12 by making the foot length shorter *(see Sizing, page 89).*

MATERIALS
Super Fine Weight Yarn
[3.5 ounces, 400 yards
(100 grams, 366 meters) per skein]:
SUPER FINE **1**
Version 1:
  A (Purple) - 1 skein
  B (Yellow) - 1 skein
  C (Green) - 1 skein
Version 2:
  A (Purple) - 1 skein
  B (Yellow) - 1 skein
Version 3:
  A (Purple) - 1 skein
Set of 4 double pointed knitting
  needles, size 2 (2.75 mm) **or** size
  needed for gauge
Split-ring marker
Tapestry needle

GAUGE: In Garter Slip Stitch
  pattern,
  14 sts and 14 rnds =
  2" (5 cm)
✓ *Take the time to check
  your gauge.*

Techniques used:
• K2 tog *(Fig. 9, page 92)*
• SSK *(Figs. 12a-c, page 92)*
• P2 tog *(Fig. 15, page 93)*

COLOR SEQUENCE

For Version 1, alternate working two rounds each of A, B and C. Drop unused color to back of work.

For Version 2, alternate working two rounds each of A and B. Drop unused color to back of work.

For Version 3, work entire Sock in A.

GARTER SLIP STITCH (multiple of 2 sts)

Rnd 1: Knit around.

Rnd 2: Purl around.

Rnd 3: ★ Slip 1 purlwise with yarn in back, K1; repeat from ★ around.

Rnd 4: ★ Slip 1 purlwise with yarn in back, P1; repeat from ★ around.

Repeat Rnds 1-4 for Garter Slip Stitch pattern.

CUFF

With A, cast on 48 sts loosely.

Divide stitches onto 3 needles, placing 16 sts on each needle.

Place a marker around the first stitch and join for working in the round, being careful not to twist stitches *(see Double Pointed Needles, page 90)*.

Work in K1, P1 ribbing for 12 rnds in color sequence.

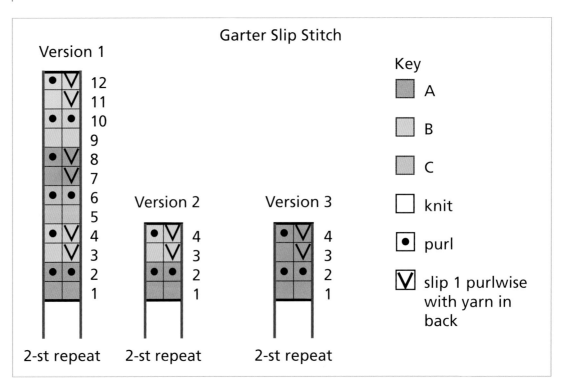

Version 2

Version 3

LEG

Continuing in color sequence, work in Garter Slip Stitch pattern until Sock measures approximately 6" (15 cm) from cast on edge, ending by working a purl rnd.

HEEL

Dividing Row: With next color, knit across Needle 1, with same needle, knit 8 sts from Needle 2; slip remaining sts from Needle 2 onto Needle 3 and leave these 24 sts unworked for Instep.

The Heel Flap will be worked back and forth in rows across the first 24 stitches.

HEEL FLAP

Continue in established color sequence on Heel Flap.

Row 1 (Wrong side): Slip 1 purlwise with yarn in front, purl across; turn.

Row 2: Slip 1 purlwise with yarn in back, knit across; turn.

Repeat Rows 1 and 2, 11 times.

HEEL TURNING

Begin working in short rows as follows, using same color as last row:

Row 1 (Wrong side): P 14, P2 tog, P1, leave remaining 7 sts unworked; turn.

Continue to slip the first stitch, holding yarn to **wrong** side, and slipping knitwise on all **right** side rows and purlwise on all **wrong** side rows.

Row 2: Slip 1, K5, SSK, K1; turn.

Row 3: Slip 1, P6, P2 tog, P1; turn.

Row 4: Slip 1, K7, SSK, K1; turn.

Row 5: Slip 1, P8, P2 tog, P1; turn.

Row 6: Slip 1, K9, SSK, K1; turn.

Row 7: Slip 1, P 10, P2 tog, P1; turn.

Row 8: Slip 1, K 11, SSK, K1; turn.

Row 9: Slip 1, P 12, P2 tog; turn.

Row 10: Slip 1, K 12, SSK: 14 sts.

Continued on page 82.

GARTER SLIP STITCH SOCKS
continued from page 81.

GUSSET

Work 2 rnds with same color as Heel Turning, then continue working in color sequence. The bottom of the Foot is worked in Stockinette Stitch while the Instep continues with the Garter Slip Stitch pattern.

Rnd 1: With **right** side of Heel facing and using needle holding Heel sts (Needle 1), pick up 12 sts along edge of Heel Flap *(Fig. 17, page 93)*, pick up one st in gap between Heel Flap and Instep; with empty needle, work 24 Instep sts in established Garter Slip Stitch pattern (Needle 2); with empty needle, pick up one st in gap between Instep and Heel Flap, pick up 12 sts along edge of Heel Flap, knit first 7 sts of Heel from Needle 1 (Needle 3), place marker around next st to indicate beginning of rnd: 64 sts, arranged 20-24-20.

Rnd 2 (Decrease rnd): On Needle 1, knit across needle to last 3 sts, K2 tog, K1; on Needle 2, work across in established Garter Slip Stitch pattern; on Needle 3, K1, SSK, knit across: 62 sts.

Rnds 3 and 4: Work around in patterns.

Repeat Rnds 2-4, 7 times: 48 sts, arranged 12-24-12.

FOOT

Work even until Foot measures approximately 7" (18 cm) from back of Heel, **or** about 2" (5 cm) shorter than desired length of Sock.

TOE

Rnd 1 (Decrease rnd): On Needle 1, knit across needle to last 3 sts, K2 tog, K1; on Needle 2, K1, SSK, knit across needle to last 3 sts, K2 tog, K1; on Needle 3, K1, SSK, knit across: 44 sts.

Rnd 2: Knit around.

Repeat Rnds 1 and 2, 5 times: 24 sts.

Repeat Rnd 1 only, 3 times: 12 sts.

FINISHING

With Needle 3, knit sts from Needle 1: 6 sts on both needles.

With tapestry needle, graft Toe *(Figs. 18a & b, page 94)*. Weave in ends.

CABLE RIB SOCKS continued from page 77.

TOE

Rnd 1 (Decrease rnd): On Needle 1, knit across needle to last 3 sts, K2 tog, K1; on Needle 2, K1, SSK, knit across needle to last 3 sts, K2 tog, K1; on Needle 3, K1, SSK, knit across: 56 sts.

Rnd 2: Knit around.

Repeat Rnds 1 and 2, 6 times: 32 sts.

Repeat Rnd 1 only, 5 times: 12 sts.

FINISHING

With Needle 3, knit sts from Needle 1: 6 sts on both needles.

With tapestry needle, graft Toe *(Figs. 18a & b, page 94)*. Weave in ends.

RIGHT SOCK
LEG

Cast on 60 sts loosely.

Divide stitches evenly onto 3 needles, placing 20 on each.

Place a marker around the first stitch and join for working in the round, being careful not to twist stitches.

To work 3/3 LC *(3 over 3 Left Cross; uses 6 sts)*, slip next 3 sts onto cable needle and hold in **front** of work, K3 from left needle, K3 from cable needle.

Rnds 1 and 2: ★ K6, P2, K2, P2; repeat from ★ around.

Rnd 3: ★ Work 3/3 LC, P2, K2, P2; repeat from ★ around.

Rnds 4-10: ★ K6, P2, K2, P2; repeat from ★ around.

Repeat Rnds 3-10 for Left Cable Rib pattern until Sock measures approximately 6" (15 cm) from cast on edge.

Beginning with Heel, complete same as Left Sock, page 76.

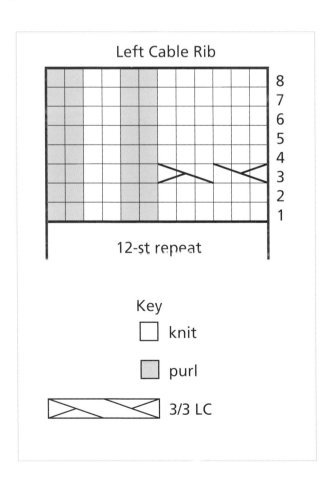

Left Cable Rib

8 7 6 5 4 3 2 1

12-st repeat

Key

☐ knit

▨ purl

⬤ 3/3 LC

TOELESS YOGA SOCKS

◖◼◻◻ **EASY +**

Size: Woman
Finished Foot Circumference: 7" (18 cm)

MATERIALS [LIGHT 3]
Light Weight Yarn
[1.75 ounces, 100 yards
(50 grams, 91 meters) per ball]:
  2 balls
Set of 4 double pointed knitting
  needles, size 3 (3.25 mm) **or**
  size needed for gauge
Split-ring marker
Tapestry needle

GAUGE: In Stockinette Stitch,
    15 sts and 22 rnds =
    2" (5 cm)
✓ *Take the time to check your
gauge.*

Techniques used:
• K2 tog *(Fig. 9, page 92)*

TWISTED RIB (multiple of 4 sts)
Rnds 1 and 2: ★ K2, P2; repeat from ★ around.
Rnd 3: ★ K2 tog leaving sts on left hand needle, then knit the first st again, slip both sts off needle, P2; repeat from ★ around.
Rnd 4: ★ K2, P2; repeat from ★ around.
Repeat Rnds 1-4 for Twisted Rib pattern.

Twisted Rib

```
                    4
                    3
                    2
                    1
         4-st
         repeat
```

Key

☐ knit

☐ purl

◥◢ K2 tog leaving sts on left hand needle, then knit the first st again, slip both sts off needle

Sock is worked from the Foot to the Cuff.

FOOT
Cast on 52 sts loosely.

Divide stitches onto 3 needles, arranged 17-18-17.

Place a marker around the first stitch and join for working in the round, being careful not to twist stitches *(see Double Pointed Needles, page 90)*.

Work 8 rnds in Twisted Rib pattern.

Knit each round until Sock measures approximately 2½" (6.5 cm) from cast on edge.

LEG
Work Rnds 1-4 of Twisted Rib pattern.

Heel Opening: Bind off 26 sts loosely in pattern, work in established Twisted Rib pattern across: 26 sts.

Next Rnd: With **wrong** side facing, cable cast on 26 sts *(Figs. 1a & b, page 90)*, **turn**; work in established Twisted Rib pattern around.

Work 6 rnds in established Twisted Rib pattern.

Knit each round until Sock measures approximately 5" (12.5 cm) from Heel opening.

CUFF
Work 8 rnds in Twisted Rib pattern.

Bind off loosely in pattern.
Weave in ends.

ABBREVIATIONS

cm	centimeters
K	knit
Kfb	knit front and back
LC	Left Cross
M1	make one
M1-R	make one right
mm	millimeters
P	purl
Pfb	purl front and back
PSSO	pass slipped stitch(es) over
RC	Right Cross
Rnd(s)	Round(s)
s2kp	slip 2, knit, pass 2 slipped sts over knit st
SSK	slip, slip, knit
SSSK	slip, slip, slip, knit
SSSSK	slip, slip, slip, slip, knit
st(s)	stitch(es)
tbl	through back loop
tog	together
w&t	wrap and turn
YO	yarn over

★ — work instructions following ★ as many **more** times as indicated in addition to the first time.

† to † — work all instructions from first † to second † **as many** times as specified.

( ) or [ ] — work enclosed instructions **as many** times as specified by the number immediately following **or** contains explanatory remarks.

colon (:) — the number(s) given after a colon at the end of a row or round denote(s) the number of stitches you should have on that row or round.

work even — work without increasing or decreasing in the established pattern.

KNIT TERMINOLOGY	
UNITED STATES	**INTERNATIONAL**
gauge =	tension
bind off =	cast off
yarn over (YO) =	yarn forward (yfwd) **or** yarn around needle (yrn)

Yarn Weight Symbol & Names	LACE 0	SUPER FINE 1	FINE 2	LIGHT 3	MEDIUM 4	BULKY 5	SUPER BULKY 6
Type of Yarns in Category	Fingering, size 10 crochet thread	Sock, Fingering, Baby	Sport, Baby	DK, Light Worsted	Worsted, Afghan, Aran	Chunky, Craft, Rug	Bulky, Roving
Knit Gauge Range* in Stockinette St to 4" (10 cm)	33-40** sts	27-32 sts	23-26 sts	21-24 sts	16-20 sts	12-15 sts	6-11 sts
Advised Needle Size Range	000-1	1 to 3	3 to 5	5 to 7	7 to 9	9 to 11	11 and larger

*GUIDELINES ONLY: The chart above reflects the most commonly used gauges and needle sizes for specific yarn categories.

** Lace weight yarns are usually knitted on larger needles to create lacy openwork patterns. Accordingly, a gauge range is difficult to determine. Always follow the gauge stated in your pattern.

KNITTING NEEDLES																
U.S.	0	1	2	3	4	5	6	7	8	9	10	10½	11	13	15	17
U.K.	13	12	11	10	9	8	7	6	5	4	3	2	1	00	000	---
Metric - mm	2	2.25	2.75	3.25	3.5	3.75	4	4.5	5	5.5	6	6.5	8	9	10	12.75

■□□□ BEGINNER	Projects for first-time knitters using basic knit and purl stitches. Minimal shaping.
■■□□ EASY	Projects using basic stitches, repetitive stitch patterns, simple color changes, and simple shaping and finishing.
■■■□ INTERMEDIATE	Projects with a variety of stitches, such as basic cables and lace, simple intarsia, double-pointed needles and knitting in the round needle techniques, mid-level shaping and finishing.
■■■■ EXPERIENCED	Projects using advanced techniques and stitches, such as short rows, fair isle, more intricate intarsia, cables, lace patterns, and numerous color changes.

SIZING

When deciding which size to make, consider the fit of a sock. As long as the socks are made from a yarn with elasticity, the fabric will have some give. You want the socks to fit snugly, but not so tight that you'll have a hard time getting them on or that the stitches are stretched out.

Measure the foot you are knitting for with a tape measure, pulling the tape snugly. Subtract 1/2" (1.5 cm), and pick the size with the foot circumference closest to this total (if the total falls exactly between two sizes, use the larger one). You can also adjust the circumference by slightly adjusting the gauge by changing needle size.

The Leg length is from the top of the sock to the top of the Heel and can also be adjusted by working more or less rounds.

The Foot length can also be adjusted before beginning the toe. The length is measured from the back of the Heel, not the spot where the heel meets the gusset. To adjust the foot length, measure the total length of the foot that will be wearing the sock. Subtract the measurement given for the toe. Work the foot to this measurement.

Most of the socks written for women can easily be made to fit a child ages 10-12 by making the foot length 1" to 1 1/2" (2.5 cm to 4 cm) shorter. And the largest child's size can be made 1" to 1 1/2" (2.5 cm to 4 cm) longer to make a woman's sock.

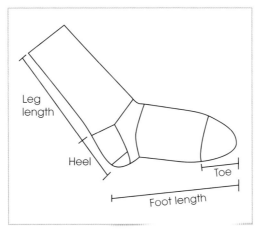

GAUGE

Exact gauge is **essential** for proper fit. Before beginning your project, make a sample swatch in the yarn and needle specified in the individual instructions. After completing the swatch, measure it, counting your stitches and rounds/rows carefully. If your swatch is larger or smaller than specified, **make another, changing needle size to get the correct gauge**. Keep trying until you find the size needles that will give you the specified gauge.

ZEROS

To consolidate the length of an involved pattern, zeros are sometimes used so that all sizes can be combined. For example, K 0{3} means the first size would do nothing and the second size would knit 3 sts.

CABLE CAST ON

Insert the right needle into the stitch as if to **knit**, yarn over and pull loop through, insert the left needle into the loop just worked from front to back and slip the loop onto the left needle.
★ Insert the right needle between the first and second stitch from front to back, yarn over and pull loop through *(Fig. 1a)*, insert the left needle into the loop just worked from front to back *(Fig. 1b)* and slip the loop onto the left needle. Repeat from ★ for required number of stitches.

Fig. 1a

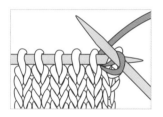

Fig. 1b

DOUBLE POINTED KNITTING NEEDLES

Divide the stitches into thirds and slip one-third of the stitches onto each of 3 double pointed needles *(Fig. 2a)*; form a triangle. With the fourth needle, knit across the stitches on the first needle *(Fig. 2b)*. You will now have an empty needle with which to knit the stitches from the next needle. Work the first stitch of each needle firmly to prevent gaps.

Fig. 2a

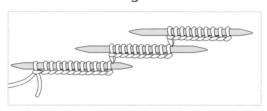

Fig. 2b

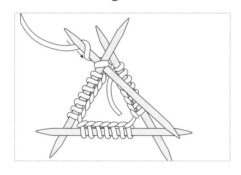

Fig. 2c

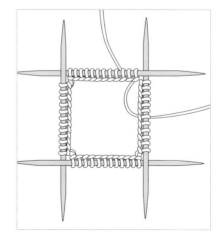

Socks worked from the Toe up require stitches placed on 4 double pointed needles. Divide the stitches evenly forming a square *(Fig. 2c)*.

Place a marker around the first stitch to indicate the beginning of the round. You may use purchased split-ring markers or place a length of contrasting color yarn around the stitch. Move it up at the end of each round.

FOLLOWING A CHART

Many of the Sock instructions include a chart as well as the written instructions for a pattern stitch. The chart shows each stitch as a square indicating what each stitch should be *(see Sample Chart, page 91)*. Visualize the chart as your fabric, beginning at the bottom edge, to help you see what the pattern looks like. Only one pattern repeat is given on the chart. This section is to be repeated across the round.

When you are knitting in the round, always follow the chart from right to left. Since the Leaf for the Leaf Sock is worked in rows, on right side rows follow the chart from right to left and on wrong side rows follow the chart from left to right.

For ease in following the chart, place a ruler or sticky note on the chart **above** the row being worked to help keep your place and allow you to see the round you have just completed. You want to know immediately if your pattern is off.

SAMPLE CHART

Eyelet Squares

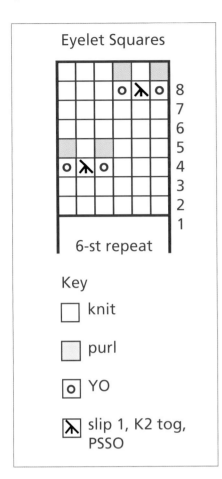

6-st repeat

Key

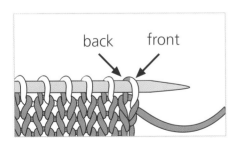

knit

purl

YO

slip 1, K2 tog, PSSO

THROUGH BACK LOOP
(abbreviated tbl)

When instructed to knit or purl into the back loop of a stitch *(Fig. 3)*, the result will be a twisted stitch.

Fig. 3

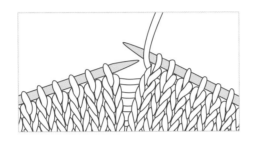

YARN OVER
(abbreviated YO)

Bring the yarn forward between the needles, then back over the top of the right hand needle, so that it is now in position to knit the next stitch *(Fig. 4)*.

Fig. 4

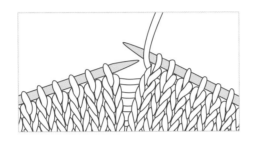

MAKE ONE
(abbreviated M1)

Insert the left hand needle under the horizontal strand between the stitches from the **front** *(Fig. 5a)*. Then knit into the **back** of the strand *(Fig. 5b)*.

Fig. 5a

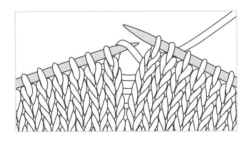

Fig. 5b

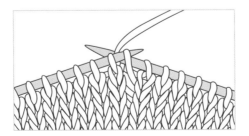

MAKE ONE RIGHT
(abbreviated M1-R)

Insert the left hand needle under the horizontal strand between the stitches from the **back** *(Fig. 6a)*. Then knit into the **front** of the strand *(Fig. 6b)*.

Fig. 6a

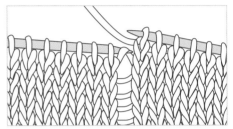

Fig. 6b

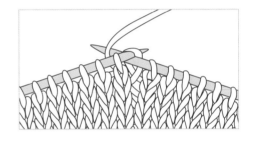

RIGHT LIFTED INCREASE

Insert the right hand needle from the **front** into the right leg of the stitch **below** the next stitch on the left hand needle *(Fig. 7)* and knit this stitch.

Fig. 7

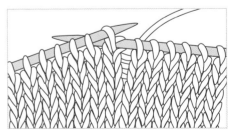

LEFT LIFTED INCREASE

Insert the left hand needle from the **back** into the left leg of the stitch 2 rows **below** the last stitch on the right hand needle *(Fig. 8a)*, pull it up and knit into the back loop *(Fig. 8b)*.

Fig. 8a

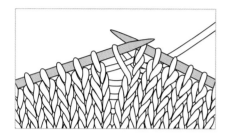

Fig. 8b

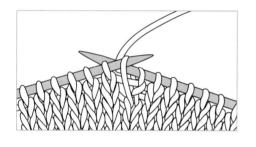

KNIT 2 TOGETHER
(abbreviated K2 tog)

Insert the right hand needle into the **front** of the first two stitches on the left hand needle as if to knit *(Fig. 9)*, then **knit** them together as if they were one stitch.

Fig. 9

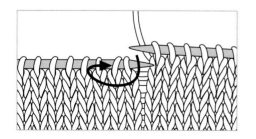

KNIT 3 TOGETHER
(abbreviated K3 tog)

Insert the right hand needle into the **front** of the first three stitches on the left hand needle as if to **knit** *(Fig. 10)*, then **knit** them together as if they were one stitch.

Fig. 10

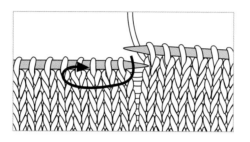

KNIT 4 TOGETHER
(abbreviated K4 tog)

Insert the right hand needle into the **front** of the first four stitches on the left hand needle as if to **knit** *(Fig. 11)*, then **knit** them together as if they were one stitch.

Fig. 11

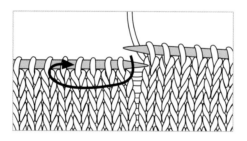

SLIP, SLIP, KNIT
(abbreviated SSK)

Separately slip two stitches as if to **knit** *(Fig. 12a)*. Insert the left hand needle into the front of both slipped stitches *(Fig. 12b)* and **knit** them together as if they were one stitch *(Fig. 12c)*.

Fig. 12a

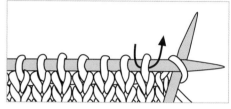

Fig. 12b

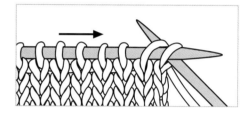

Fig. 12c

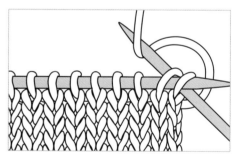

SLIP 1, KNIT 1, PASS SLIPPED STITCH OVER

Slip one stitch as if to **knit**. Knit the next stitch. With the left hand needle, bring the slipped stitch over the knit stitch just made *(Fig. 13)* and off the needle.

Fig. 13

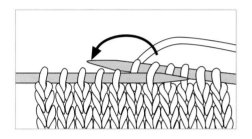

SLIP 1, KNIT 2 TOGETHER, PASS SLIPPED STITCH OVER

Slip one stitch as if to **knit**. Knit the next 2 stitches together *(Fig. 9)*. With the **left** hand needle, bring the slipped stitch over the stitch just made *(Fig. 14)* and off the needle.

Fig. 14

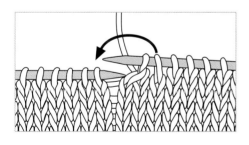

PURL 2 TOGETHER
(abbreviated P2 tog)

Insert the right hand needle into the **front** of the first two stitches on the left hand needle as if to **purl** *(Fig. 15)*, then **purl** them together as if they were one stitch.

Fig. 15

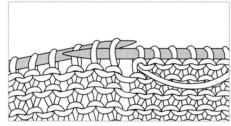

TAPESTRY NEEDLE BIND OFF

This produces a very stretchy bind off that is great for socks. Thread a tapestry needle with a long end. ★ Insert the tapestry needle through the first 2 stitches as if to **purl**, then through the first stitch as if to **knit** *(Fig. 16)* slipping the first stitch off the left needle; repeat from ★ across.

Fig. 16

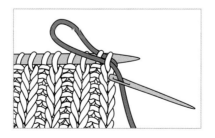

PICKING UP STITCHES

When instructed to pick up stitches, insert the needle from the **front** to the **back** under two strands at the edge of the worked piece *(Fig. 17)*. Put the yarn around the needle as if to **knit**, then bring the needle with the yarn back through the stitch to the right side, resulting in a stitch on the needle.
Repeat this along the edge, picking up the required number of stitches.

A crochet hook may be helpful to pull yarn through.

Fig. 17

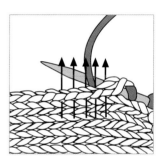

GRAFTING

Stitches to be woven are held on two knitting needles, with one behind the other and **wrong** sides together. Threaded tapestry needle should be on the right hand side of the work. Work in the following sequence, pulling yarn through as if to **knit** or as if to **purl** with even tension and keeping yarn under the points of the needles to avoid tangling and extra loops.

Step 1: Purl first stitch on **front** needle, leave on *(Fig. 18a)*.

Step 2: Knit first stitch on **back** needle, leave on *(Fig. 18b)*.

Step 3: Knit first stitch on **front** needle, slip off.

Step 4: Purl next stitch on **front** needle, leave on.

Step 5: Purl first stitch on **back** needle, slip off.

Step 6: Knit next stitch on **back** needle, leave on.

Repeat Steps 3-6 across until one st remains on each needle, then repeat Steps 3 and 5.

Fig. 18a

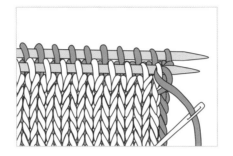

Fig. 18b

BLOCKING

Check the yarn label for any special instructions about blocking. For Socks made with wool yarn, a handheld steamer or a steam iron works well. Place your project on a clean terry towel over a flat surface and shape it to size; pin it in place using rust-proof pins if needed. Being careful not to put a crease at the sides, hold a steamer or steam iron just above the item and steam it thoroughly. Never let the weight of the iron touch the item because it will flatten the stitches. Allow the item to dry flat, away from heat or sunlight.

YARN INFORMATION

The socks in this leaflet were made using a variety of yarns. Any brand of the specific weight of yarn may be used. It is best to refer to the yardage/meters when determining how many balls or skeins to purchase. Remember, to arrive at the finished size, it is the GAUGE/TENSION that is important, not the brand of yarn.

For your convenience, listed below are the specific yarns used to create our photography models.

BRIGHT TWEED SOCKS
Shibui Knits Sock Yarn
(A) #1797 Chinese Red
(B) #021 Lily

BRAIDED CABLE SOCKS
Premier™ Yarns
Deborah Norville
Collection™ Serenity™ Sock
Weight Solids
#DN150-07 Woodsy Green

CHEVRON PURLS SOCKS
Lion Brand® LB Collection®
Superwash Merino
#107 Sky

HEART TOE-UP SOCKS
Claudia Hand Painted Yarns
Fingering
Peony

EYELET TOE-UP SOCKS
Claudia Hand Painted Yarns
Fingering
Honey

KNOTTED RIB SOCKS
Plymouth Yarn® Sockin' Sox
#004 brown/tan multi

SEED STRIPES SOCKS
Knit One Crochet Too
TY-DY Socks Dots
#6985 Putty

TWO-RIBBED SOCKS
Lion Brand® Sock-Ease™
#100 Marshmallow

TINY TOES SOCKS
Cleckheaton Cocoon
#0003

BABY RIB SOCKS
Lorna's Laces Shepherd Sock
Clara's Garden

SIMPLE SLIP STITCH SOCKS
Patons® Kroy Socks
#55617 Sporty Stripes

EYELET SQUARES SOCKS
Lorna's Laces Shepherd Sock
#37ns Violet

BUTTERFLY BOWS SOCKS
Lion Brand® LB Collection®
Superwash Merino
#139 Peony

SPIRAL RIB SOCKS
Version 1:
Red Heart® Heart & Sole™
#3960 Spring Stripe

Version 2:
Premier™ Yarns
Deborah Norville Collection™
Serenity™ Sock Weight Solids
#DN150-02 Hot Pink

LEAF SOCK
Plymouth Yarn®
Happy Feet DK
#63 multi

CABLE RIB SOCKS
Shibui Knits Sock Yarn
#340 Kiwi

GARTER SLIP STITCH SOCKS
Alpaca With a Twist Socrates
Version 1:
(A) #2016 Laura's Purple
(B) #5017 Jennifer's Yellow
(C) #4018 Wednesday Night
    Green

Version 2:
(A) #2016 Laura's Purple
(B) #5017 Jennifer's Yellow

Version 3:
(A) #2016 Laura's Purple

TOELESS YOGA SOCKS
Cascade Yarns Fixation
#4447 (Orange)

Instructions tested and photo models made by Ruth Arnold, Nancy Desmarais, Raymelle Greening, Barbara Kreuter, Dale Potter, Ted Tomany, Claudia Wittmann, and Catherine Wingfield-Yeatts.